# SŌSEKI NATSUME'S
## Collected HAIKU

**1,000 VERSES FROM JAPAN'S MOST POPULAR WRITER**

*translated and introduced by*
### ERIK R. LOFGREN

TUTTLE Publishing
Tokyo | Rutland, Vermont | Singapore

# Contents

Acknowledgments

v

Introduction

**vii**

A Note on the Translations

**xv**

## THE POEMS

New Year's

**1**

Spring

**9**

Summer

**89**

Autumn

**127**

Winter

**217**

No Season

**277**

Notes

**282**

# Acknowledgments

Elizabeth Armstrong, my wife and colleague, who is an accomplished translator in her own right, served as a sounding board and inspiration throughout the process of writing this book, offering myriad valuable suggestions and not a few apposite criticisms. It is largely through her example that I was able to undertake and bring to fruition this project.

My colleagues in the East Asian Studies department have been more helpful than I had any right to hope. Song Chen and Yunjing Xu provided valuable assistance with some of the details of classical Chinese history and literature, entirely familiar to Sōseki, but certainly less so to me. Jim Orr was, as he always is, a steady presence and an exemplary colleague.

The website *sosekihaikushu* <sosekihaikushu.at.webry.info/> constructed and maintained by Kitayama Masaji was an invaluable resource for readings and context for certain poems. Among the site's many strengths are its several indices: a chronological listing, a listing by *kigo* (seasonal word), and a phonetic listing.

During a stint teaching for the Associated Kyoto Program in 2019–20, Mari Kawata, the Program's Office Director, facilitated an essential connection with Ryōsuke Deki whose guidance with particularly thorny constructions was invaluable. I was also fortunate to be able to lean on several students for assistance. Quinn Audouin helped reduce the burden of proofreading the transliterations in the early stage of editing, and Sofija Podvisocka and Matthew Rosenberg were able to locate an obscure reference.

Bucknell University provided a sabbatical and funding that gave me the time to complete the first draft of the translations.

Dean's Travel Funds allowed me to attend the Middlebury Bread Loaf Translators' Conference in June 2021. My colleagues at that conference—Ana Ban, Chloe Farrell, Heather Green, Natalie Harty, Cindy Juyoung Ok, and Karen Emmerich who served as our mentor—were gracious with their time and insightful in their feedback. Time and again I have had occasion to reflect upon their observations to the benefit of the translations, I hope.

Gerry Wilson helped launch me on this wondrous journey some four decades ago. Carol Armstrong has long been an inspiration. Our children, Rebekah and Mariah Lofgren, have been bemused cheerleaders over the years. Finally, Molly Lofgren has been a steadfast supporter in ways immeasurable despite all the tribulations a son might sling her way.

---

To Access Online Audios & Indexes:

1. Check to be sure you have an Internet connection.
2. Type the URL below into your web browser.

https://www.tuttlepublishing.com/
soseki-natsume-collected-haiku

For support, you can email us at info@tuttlepublishing.com

# Introduction

Sōseki Natsume (1867–1916) was born the year before the curtain came down on the Edo period (1600–1868) and Japan embarked on a wholesale effort to "modernize" by means of a vigorous borrowing of Western models: military and political structures, banking and postal systems, literary modes, and a host of others. Sōseki's education reflected this bifurcated sense of national identity in that he was given the best of both worlds. Trained in the classics of Chinese and Japanese litera-

ture and thought, he was also schooled in those subjects deemed important to national advancement, including English which eventually led him to spend an unpleasant two years in London absorbing western literary learning. Upon his return to Japan in 1903, he took up a post at Tokyo Imperial University where he taught English literature. Two years later saw the publication of Sōseki's first novel, *I am a Cat* (*Wagahai wa neko de aru*, 1905–06). The surprising success of this work began an internal struggle focused on possible routes forward: educator or novelist. The latter eventually triumphed and in 1907, after a mere four years in what was a very prestigious position, he tendered his resignation and joined the Asahi Newspaper, a job with a significantly lower social status. It did, however, give Sōseki a place to expand his novelistic output, and the pay was much better which meant he was free to focus on his writing. By the time of his death ten years later, Sōseki had penned a dozen novels and numerous collections of short stories, firmly establishing his place in the literary pantheon as one of the greats of modern Japanese literature.

Although it is largely as a novelist that Sōseki is remembered, he was also an avid poet, writing in numerous modes from the time he was in middle school until his death. In that 35-year period, he wrote thousands of poems, the bulk of which were *haiku*. Although to the extent that people associate Sōseki with poetry, it is with classical Chinese poetry (*kanshi*) that they do so, his tremendous output of *haiku* commends our attention for the light they shine on this venerated author.

It was no easy task to choose which 1,000 to include from the 2,560 that are present in his most recent *Soseki zenshu* (*Collected works*), if for no other reason than there were no obviously satisfactory criteria. I did not want something that reflected a particular season or specific theme, nor did I really want just "the best" poems I could find. Indeed, determining "the best" in something as subjective as poetry is an enterprise doomed to failure before its start.

*viii*

As one might expect, their quality is uneven. In the end, I chose simply to privilege those poems that spoke to me in some way. Sōseki's *haiku* run the gamut from the elegant to the crude, the somber to the playful, the refined to the banal. This collection strives to give voice to this diversity, and I have tried to select those that are representative in terms of theme and tone, as well as those that captivate or excite the reader, and those that may be less successful by whatever measure. I have also included as curiosities a few that, by virtue of simple passage of time, have lost whatever impact they might have had as their subjects have faded into the dusts of obscurity.

This collection contains *haiku* from every year in which Sōseki wrote them, although there were slim pickings from some years—1889 and 1892, for example, saw only two poems, and he seems to have written none in 1893. Sōseki appears not to have found solace in composing *haiku* during his years in London for few date from those years, as well. Finally, numerous scholars have remarked that the majority of his *haiku* (about 70%) were written in the first half of Sōseki's years as a productive *haiku* poet, or while his long-time friend and mentor, Shiki Masaoka (1867–1902) was still alive. These scholars seem to imply that Sōseki was writing largely for Shiki. To be sure, he sent a substantial number of his compositions to Shiki for evaluation; however, the fact that roughly 30% were written after Shiki died suggests that Sōseki was not writing *haiku* solely for Shiki, nor that his interest in the form dwindled precipitously after 1902. In other words, whatever value or pleasure he got from their creation was a lifelong companion.

Sōseki got to know Shiki in school in 1888 and the two quickly formed a deep and lasting friendship. This suggests the value of taking a small detour into Shiki's life. His influence on modern *haiku* cannot be overstated. In 1897 he founded the long-lived literary magazine *Hototogisu* which became the leading forum for his Nippon school of *haiku*. Shiki sought to challenge the dominant traditional requirements of the form by emphasizing the importance of inspiration gleaned from personal experiences of nature. The effect of his mentorship for Sōseki is equally noteworthy; however, in much the same way Sōseki's novels would hew not to current literary fads but, rather, to his own sensibility, so too were his *haiku* not simply the product of applying Shiki's formulations. Considered as a whole, Sōseki's *haiku oeuvre* might be seen in aggregate as more personal and, perhaps, playful. For example, he often used this poetic form to express his inner concerns, or to poke fun at something, or to laugh at some of the absurdities in life. That said, the earliest *haiku* he wrote of which we have a record were in a letter to his new friend, Shiki Masaoka, who had been stricken with tuberculosis. Sōseki urged him to get well soon and included two *haiku*. It is thought that Sōseki wrote them after visiting the convalescing patient and, subsequently, talking with his physician.

There are two major events in Sōseki's life that deserve particular mention because of their manifestation in his *haiku*. The first was a two-year sojourn to London resulting from an official order in 1900 from the Ministry of Education to study English as an exchange student. This was, in part, due to his existing proficiency in the language. Indeed, almost a decade before his time in England Sōseki produced a solid translation of the thirteenth-century classic *Hōjōki* (Tales of My Ten Foot Square Hut) which showcases his already-impressive talent for writing in English. This facility notwithstanding, Sōseki tried to get out of this responsibility to his country, but he was unsuccessful. He departed Japan in September 1900 and left England in December 1902 to finally disembark on Japanese soil once again in late January 1903. A great deal has been written elsewhere about Sōseki's time in England and its effect on his future literary career. One outcome related tangentially to this collection of poetry is that Sōseki also wrote some

INTRODUCTION

essays and a handful of poems in English. We ought not to be surprised by this given his long interest in writing poetry in Japanese and Chinese. Leaving aside the question of quality—a fraught determination with poetry in the best of cases—it is interesting to see in his English verse some resonances of the themes, images, and, perhaps, brevity, that we see in his *haiku*. Take, for example, this poem written in November 1903:

I looked at her as she looked at me:
We looked and stood a moment,
Between Life and Dream.

We never met since:
Yet oft I stand
In the primrose path
Where Life meets Dream.

Oh that Life could
Melt into Dream
Instead of Dream
Is constantly
Chased away by Life!

We might recognize in it a well-worn trope of the mutability between life and dream seen across the centuries of Japanese poetry, and the frustration that accompanies that unstable intersection. Another poem, undated although we might suppose it was written while Sōseki was in London, foregrounds crickets and loneliness, both of which appear in Sōseki's *haiku* as well.

*xi*

Lonely I sit in my lonesome chamber
 And cricket chirps.
My lamp lies lonely half in slumber
 And cricket chirps.

Soul, in dim conscious delight
 In cricket chirps,
Lost and forlorn, forlorn and bright
 With cricket chirps.

Is it my soul or only cricket
That chirps so lonely in my chamber?
 still cricket chirps,
 Chirping
 Chin—chi—ro—rin.

Although Sōseki abandoned English as a medium for poetry, he did write one more poem soon after his return to Japan. It is a flawed and not terribly upbeat work. In it, we may glean hints of some of the underlying tensions in Sōseki's life.

We live in different worlds, you and I.
Try what means you will,
We cannot meet, you and I.
You live in your world and are happy;
I in mine and am contented.
Then let us understand better
Not to interfere with each other's lot.
We break an ox's horn by bending it;
We are not meant to be broken like that!

*xii*

Your world is far away from me.
It is veiled with miles of mist and haze.
It is in vain the I should strain my eyes
To catch glimpses of your abode.
Flowers may there be; and lots of things pretty,
Yet never in a dream I wished to be there.
For I am here and not there;
And I am forever mine and not yours!

The second important event was a very serious ailment in that came to a head in 1910. Sōseki had been complaining of stomach problems, a condition that was diagnosed as probable stomach ulcers in the summer of that year. After a protracted stay in the hospital, his condition improved, and he decided to spend some time at Shuzenji convalescing. A short while after his arrival in early August, his health took a sharp turn for the worse. His condition was so dire that contingency plans were made in the event of his death. The month that he had planned to be there stretched into two, but at the end of that time he was again out of danger. This near-death experience finds outlet in both his *haiku* and his *kanshi* written at this time. The illness, however, was his constant companion until the fifth recurrence led to his death in 1916.

## FURTHER READING

Beichman, Janine. *Masaoka Shiki: His Life and Works.* Cheng and Tsui, 2002.

Gessel, Van C. *Three Modern Novelists: Sōseki, Tanizaki, Kawabata.* Kodansha International, 1993.

Nathan, John. *Sōseki: Modern Japan's Greatest Novelist.* Columbia UP, 2018.

Sato, Hiroaki. *On Haiku.* New Directions, 2018.

# A Note on the Translations

I have arranged the poems by the five traditional seasons and the null category: new year's, spring, summer, autumn, winter, and no specified season. Within those groups, the poems are arranged chronologically in the order they appear in *Sōseki zenshū* (2019; henceforth SZ). Readers interested in the date, or the season word(s) are directed to the online index available online (see page vi for details of access). There, one can also find the number of the poem as it is listed in SZ which will provide access to the minimal commentary included in that collection as well as the specifics of where the poems first appeared (collections sent to Shiki for his evaluation, in letters or on postcards to friends, in other works written by Sōseki, etc.).

It is readily apparent that I have adopted an eclectic stance toward just about every aspect of the translation process. This is most obviously visible in the lineation. In the West, we have a long poetic tradition that privileges lines, often grouped into stanzas. Since Japanese poetry first began to appear in English translation, this domestic tradition was imposed upon the foreign source. Indeed, the very way we describe Japanese poetry in terms of chunked syllable counts and breaks—5-7-5-7-7 for *waka* (*tanka*), from which *haiku* developed, and 5-7-5 for *haiku*—rather than total syllable count—35 and 17, respectively—effects a somewhat artificial division that has historically manifested itself in a 5-line form for *waka* and 3-line form for *haiku*. Compounding the artificiality of the lineation is the fact that in the original, these poems are overwhelmingly written as a single line.

Fundamentally, I am in favor of a two-line rendering of *haiku*

*xv*

into English because that seems the easiest way to express a linguistic element found in many of these poems that has no easy equivalent in English: the *kireji* (cutting word) or caesura. When present, the caesura divides the *haiku* into two parts that exist seemingly independent of each other, bound only by a term that marks their separation. In the vast majority of these cases, two lines delivers visually what is a struggle linguistically. There are some cases, however, when I felt the poem actually embedded three distinct components. In those cases, a three-line translation better captures what is going on in the original. By the same token, Sōseki wrote some *haiku* that almost seem to auger the advent of free verse. These poems feel more like a rumination on a topic. As such, there is no obvious way to determine a line break (aside, of course, from following the time-worn convention of syllable count which I have already dismissed as a hard and fast guiding principle). In these instances, I have opted to retain the original single-line form. Neither the two-line nor single-line form is new. Although the bulk of published *haiku* translations cleave to the three-line pattern, examples of the alternatives I am using are readily available.

I also chose not to be slave to syllable[1] counts, although there are times when my translation does, coincidentally, have the same number of syllables as the original; rather, I was guided by the overarching sense of brevity that that syllable count enforces. It is worth pointing out that although *haiku* usually have 17 syllables, it is not uncommon for a poet to include an extra syllable or two. This is called *ji-amari*, excess characters. Sōseki, too, wrote any number of *haiku* that exhibit this excess and, on rare occasions, to a surprising degree. For example:

---

1 It would be technically correct to use "mora" instead of "syllable" because the matter of duration is essential in the pronunciation of Japanese; however, the use of the latter is so broadly accepted that I am comfortable continuing that practice here.

*xvi*

# A NOTE ON THE TRANSLATIONS

> the spirit of a plum is a beautiful woman
> > the spirit of a pine is an old man

梅の精は美人にて松の精は翁也
*ume no sei wa bijin nite matsu no sei wa okina nari*

This has an astonishing 22 syllables structured in a 6-5-6-5 pattern. Some might question whether it should be called a *haiku* at all, but Sōseki evidently believed it was.

Many times—although not always—the power of *haiku* derives from their economy. I have, therefore, striven to be economical, regardless of the syllable count in the original. On the other hand, that economy in Japanese is aided by a language marked by myriad words which, despite their brevity, encode fairly complex ideas that may require a disproportionally large number of syllables to render faithfully—and this is, of course, a fraught term—in English. Take, for example, *kinuginu* in:

**Love's Parting**
> the morning after;
> > the bamboo field out back is thick with mist

きぬぎぬや裏の篠原露多し
*kinuginu ya ura no shinohara kiri ōshi*

This wonderful term, four syllables in length, expresses "the morning after a couple has slept together" or "parting ways the morning after having spent the night together." In either case, we have almost an entire *haiku* worth of syllables in the English before even considering the rest of the poem!

Much has been said about the economy of *haiku* and their reliance on suggestion and association. This presents the translator with a particular struggle: how to capture those elements of the poem for an audience unfamiliar with the necessary underlying cultural and/or historical information.

hearing a Kyoto lilt ask of crimson plum blossoms
I paid the city a visit

京音の紅梅ありやと尋ねけり
*kyōon no kōbai ari ya to tazunekeri*

A great deal of the force of this poem comes from *kyōon*, translated here as "Kyoto lilt," but that is, in many ways, insufficient. A more robust rendering might be "that special cadence characteristic of Kyoto dialect." It is precisely because of the associations the Kyoto dialect has—with history, with poetry, and with cultural legacy—that the mention of plum blossoms in that voice compels the poet to visit. For example, one might recall Kitano Tenmangū, a Shinto shrine in the northern part of the city dedicated to the scholar poet Sugawara no Michizane (845–903) whose favorite tree was the plum which fill the grounds of the shrine. How does one distill all of that into fifteen syllables without recourse to the knowledge Sōseki brought to his craft?

In the same vein:

a guest with a poem
ink flows from the ground inkstick
before the moon

*xviii*

## A NOTE ON THE TRANSLATIONS

客に賦あり墨磨り流す月の前
*kyaku ni fu ari sumi surinagasu tsuki no mae*

is unsatisfying because "poem" is an impoverished reflection of *fu*. Strictly speaking, a *fu* is a poem; however, there are so many different kinds of poetry to which that broad term might apply that the English "poem" gives no sense of the specificity of the original. To be more precise, however, would render the translation far too long and stilted.

Every now and again, a poem lends itself to a translation that, strictly speaking, might stray from the original, but is still pleasing enough to warrant inclusion.

> a hard pear
>     paired with a dull paring knife

堅き梨に鈍き刃物を添てけり
*kataki nashi ni nibuki hamono o soetekeri*

Sōseki was not engaged in wordplay here for there is none of the homophony present in the English in *kataki*, *hamono*, and *soetekeri*, but the serendipity the image offered seems so much more appealing than a strictly literal:

> a hard pear
>     together with a dull knife

*xix*

The vast majority of *haiku* include a "season word" (*kigo*); some even have two. I have compiled all the season words for all the poems in this anthology online (see page vi for details of access). It is important to recognize, however, that there is only an imperfect correspondence between what we in the northern hemisphere, above a certain latitude, might think of as the season and the terms used in *haiku*. Take, for example, the term *koharu*, literally "little spring." Despite the appearance of "spring" in the term, this actually denotes "the first month of winter." Even that, however, is only an imperfect understanding. The term refers to October, when the seasons are on the cusp of changing but the weather has a spring-like warmth to it. We might think of "Indian summer" as a rough equivalent. That notwithstanding, I have chosen to render most *kigo* rather more closely to their Japanese original than to their approximate Western equivalent. Therefore, considering the example above, in poems with *koharu* in them, I privilege "first month of winter" over "October" or "Indian Summer."

As I have mentioned, Sōseki was educated in the Chinese classics, and he was an adept practitioner of *kanshi*, poetry written in classical Chinese. Consequently, his working knowledge of characters was extensive. This poses something of a conundrum for the translator. Although Sōseki was notoriously lax in his use of characters, his prodigious breadth and depth of knowledge in this area at the very least suggests the possibility of nuance difficult to convey in English. Thus, although we cannot say for certain that he intended his readers to perceive a difference between 瀧 and 瀑 (*taki*, waterfall), the fact is that he did use both. Although I might have rendered 瀧 as "cataract" and 瀑 as "waterfall," for example, I have not been consistent in following those character distinctions in deference to other considerations present in any given poem.

This laxity of character use, and its attendant implications for translation, is related, in part, to a fluidity in Japanese that allows multiple readings for characters including those that are not, strictly

A NOTE ON THE TRANSLATIONS

speaking, legitimate, but which the inherent meaning of the characters permits. An example of this in Sōseki's *haiku* is the term 温泉 ("hot springs") which is usually the four-syllable word *onsen* (o-n-se-n). In addition to this, however, Sōseki has also rendered this two-character compound as *ideyu* (i-de-yu), *deyu* (de-yu), and *yu* as the syllabification needs of the respective poem dictated. All are perfectly acceptable ways to describe "hot spring." Were I to try to follow Sōseki's variations, I might try to match an English word of similar syllable counts to each term: "mineral spring" for *onsen*, "the waters" for *ideyu*, "hot springs" for *deyu*, and "spa" for *yu*. It quickly became clear that the translations, too, required a greater degree of flexibility than close adherence to character and term usage might permit and, thus, I chose not to be strictly limited by character usage, interesting and challenging though this undoubtedly is. The Japanese original accompanies each poem and readers conversant in Japanese will certainly draw their own conclusions about my decision.

Finally, the content of the *haiku* deserves some attention. One might be tempted to see in some of his *haiku*, manifestations of Sōseki's life-long interest in *kanshi*. Where *haiku* are, traditionally, *kanji* light, Sōseki would occasionally pack his offerings with *kanji*. Take for example:

following the train
the smoke crawls languidly
o'er desolate fields

汽車を逐て煙這行枯野哉
*kisha o otte kemuri haiyuku kareno kana*

Here, only two elements are in *hiragana*: the direct object marker *o* (を) and the continuative marker *te* (て). Visually, this feels much closer to a *kanshi* than a *haiku*, although there are also obvious structural differences. We also find hints at the depth of his erudition in the subjects for some of the *haiku*:

plying the boat's oars astride a horse
    a springtime journey

馬の背で船漕ぎ出すや春の旅
*uma no se de fune kogidasu ya haru no tabi*

This recalls to mind the poem "Eight Immortals of the Wine Cup" by the great Tang Dynasty poet Du Fu (712–770). Its first line describes He Zhizhang (ca. 659–744), a poet and scholar-official, riding a horse as if he were riding a boat. As another example, critics suggest that the following poem harkens back to the Tang Dynasty poet Meng Haoran (689/691–740):

clouds here and there obscure the crags above
    brilliant autumn foliage

雲處々岩に喰ひ込む紅葉哉
*kumo achikochi iwa ni kuikomu momiji kana*

Some *haiku* are included here because of the window they offer into the period.

## A NOTE ON THE TRANSLATIONS

pitter-patter on a rubber raincoat
    autumn rain

さらさらと護謨の合羽に秋の雨
*sarasara to gomu no kappa ni aki no ame*

a snagged rubber balloon
    willow tree

引かゝる護謨風船や柳の木
*hikkakaru gomufūsen ya yanagi no ki*

It is not just a balloon or a raincoat, but one made of rubber. This connection to Western goods in 1899 or 1914, respectively, should not come as a great surprise, but the specificity of *gomu no kappa* (rubber raincoat) or *gomufūsen* (rubber balloon) still points to the difference in the material and its uses relative to the domestic counterparts.

Finally, a word on Japanese terms in the translations. There is much about Japan that is familiar to a Western audience. Sushi, udon, anime, manga: all of these enjoy a wide currency. There are certain terms, however, that are less well known, but whose rendering into English leads to either an unwieldy or infelicitous translation. I will, therefore, set forth a few terms that I have chosen to keep in their Japanese original. They do not necessarily crop up frequently; however, there are enough instances that I feel it beneficial to introduce them here.

*kotatsu*    a low table with a heating source underneath that one covers with a quilt. In winter months, this arrangement will keep one's lower body warm.

*xxiii*

| | |
|---|---|
| *koto* | a half-tube stringed instrument roughly six feet long with movable bridges under the strings. It is played by plucking. |
| *torii* | a style of gate with two vertical posts and two cross bars at the top most frequently found at the entrance to or on the grounds of a Shintō shrine. They generally mark a sacred space. |
| *mikan* | a clementine or tangerine |

## CONCLUSION

One need only look up translations the famous poem on an old pond and a frog by of Matsuo Bashō (1644–94) to realize that although *haiku* are short, the possibilities they offer for variation to translators are myriad.

> an old pond;
>   a frog jumps in
>     water sound

> 古池や蛙飛び込む水の音
> *furuike ya kawazu tobikomu mizu no oto*

Thus, I have no illusions that my translations will satisfy all readers. It is my hope, however, that at least some of the renderings offered here resonate with you and provide a window into both the production of this artform in the late-nineteenth and early-twentieth centuries, as well as the breadth of artistic capabilities of their author who was much more than just a great novelist.

# New Year's

## 新年

first dream of the year;
    neither finding money, nor dying

初夢や金も拾はず死にもせず
*hatsuyume ya kane mo hirowazu shinimosezu*

———

worldly desires reduced by 108
    New Year's morning

煩悩は百八減つて今朝の春
*bonnō wa hyaku-hachi hette kesa no haru*

———

heaven and earth in easy harmony—
    the first haze of spring

天と地の打ち解けりな初霞
*ten to chi no uchitokekeri na hatsugasumi*

SŌSEKI NATSUME'S COLLECTED HAIKU

on my hermitage
the clinging icicles also greet the new year

吾庵は氷柱も歳を迎へけり
*waga io wa tsurara mo toshi o mukaekeri*

New Year's day
longing for my parents before they were born

元日に生れぬ先の親戀し
*ganjitsu ni umarenu saki no oya koishi*[1]

New Year's Day;
I think of myself unsettled and staggering drunk

元日や蹣跚として吾思ひ
*ganjitsu ya mansan toshite waga omoi*

shall we compose poetry?
you rub the inkstick this New Year's day morn

詩を書かん君墨を磨れ今朝の春
*shi o kakan kimi sumi o sure kesa no haru*

arranging pine boughs
    the sky faintly bright through the gate

松立てゝ空ほのぼのと明る門
*matsu tatete sora honobono to akaru kado*

---

poor though I may be, *sake* is so easy to drink
    a new year

貧といへど酒飲みやすし君が春
*hin to iedo sake nomiyasushi kimi ga haru*

---

I languish in bed
    fêting the new year as the chrysanthemums wither

床の上に菊枯れながら明の春
*toko no ue ni kiku karenagara ake no haru*

a bit late, with the mountains at my back
    sunrise on New Year's

稍遅し山を背にして初日影
*yaya ososhi yama o se ni shite hatsuhikage*

dashing up the pine-covered hill;
    the year's first sunrise

馳け上る松の小山や初日の出
*kakenoboru matsu no koyama ya hatsuhinode*

*A Obama with an eye toward spring*

a hot spring;
    the warm water expunging all last year's scurf

温泉や水滑かに去年の垢
*onsen ya mizu nameraka ni kozo no aka*

# NEW YEAR'S

*During the funeral service for the Imperial personage*

this year I have foregone New Year's greetings as well
  abundant snow

此春を御慶もいはで雪多し
*kono haru o gyokei mo iwade yuki ōshi*

———

from amongst the myriad clouds
  the year's first sunrise

色々の雲の中より初日出
*iroiro no kumo no naka yori hatsuhinode*

———

*In Usa on the second day of the new year and, despite it being a new calendar, not a single house is decorated with the ceremonial "gate pines"*

entering a desolate, old train station;
  eventide in the new year

蕭條たる古驛に入るや春の夕
*shōjōtaru koeki ni iru ya haru no yū*

a day late with supplications and prayers
    New Year's

ぬかづいて曰く正月二日なり
*nukazuite iwaku shōgatsu futsuka nari*

---

moss on the pines as the cranes waste away
    celebrating the new year

松の苔鶴痩せながら神の春
*matsu no koke tsuru yasenagara kami no haru*

---

in bloom on a folding screen by Kōrin;
    Amur adonis

光琳の屏風に咲くや福壽草
*Kōrin no byōbu ni saku ya fukujusō*[2]

---

kicked by a horse
    I collapsed in the blizzard

馬に蹴られ吹雪の中に倒れけり
*uma ni kerare fubuki no naka ni taorekeri*

# NEW YEAR'S

a stone sent skipping with hollow reverberations
  across the ice

石打てばかららんと鳴る氷哉
*ishi uteba kararan to naru kōri kana*

a Zen acolyte and a fluttering flag—
  spring breeze

禪僧に旛動きけり春の風
*zensō ni hata ugokikeri haru no kaze*[3]

auspicious New Year's rain
  tranquil alcove;
    Kohōgen

御降に閑なる床や古法眼
*osagari ni kan naru toko ya Kohōgen*[4]

so many bridges across the Kamo River
  spring breeze

加茂にわたす橋の多さよ春の風
*Kamo ni watasu hashi no ōsa yo haru no kaze*

# Spring

## 春

the vernal east wind blows;
    mountains fully in cloud shadow

東風吹くや山一ぱいの雲の影
*kochi fuku ya yama ippai no kumo no kage*

plying the boat's oars astride a horse
    a springtime journey

馬の背で船漕ぎ出すや春の旅
*uma no se de fune kogidasu ya haru no tabi*[1]

a gentle spring rain;
    damp, I wend my way through weeping willows

春雨や柳の中のを濡れて行く
*harusame ya yanagi no naka no o nurete yuku*

a mighty longbow;
    fluttering, fluttering, fall the plum blossoms

大弓やひらりひらりと梅の花
*ōyumi ya hirarihirari to ume no hana*

---

a passing arrow's faint sigh
    amidst plum blossoms

矢響の只聞ゆなり梅の中
*yahibiki no tada kikoyu nari ume no naka*

---

at the bowstring's twang
    a camellia blossom drops languidly

弦音にほたりと落る椿かな
*tsuruoto ni hotari to ochiru tsubaki kana*

---

gentle spring rain;
    supine, I look to my side at the plum blossoms

春雨や寐ながら横に梅を見る
*harusame ya nenagara yoko ni ume o miru*

## SPRING

riding the wind,
    gently urged forward
        a swallow

風に乗つて輕くのし行く燕かな
*kaze ni notte karuku noshiyuku tsubame kana*

---

a small dipper;
    the butterfly's pilgrimage
        here to there for its young

小柄杓や蝶を追ひおひ子順禮
*kobishaku ya chō o oioi ko junrei*

---

has a bird come?
    flower shadows shift on the paper screen

鳥や來て障子に動く花の影
*tori ya kite shōji ni ugoku hana no kage*

just after midnight
   the acolyte leaves
      plum trees in the moonlight

夜三更僧去つて梅の月夜かな
*yoru sankō sō satte ume no tsukiyo kana*

---

they are cherry blossoms
   how exquisitely they scatter

名は櫻物の見事に散る事よ
*na wa sakura mono no migoto ni chiru koto yo*

tomcat in heat;
 a husband is no match

戀猫や主人は心地例ならず
*koineko ya shujin wa kokochi rei narazu*

---

wordless epiphany
 a single white plum in bloom

不立文字白梅一木咲きにけり
*furyūmoji hakubai ichiboku sakinikeri*

---

genial spring breeze;
 a female pack-horse driver
  what tune does she sing?

春風や女の馬子の何歌ふ
*harukaze ya onna no mago no nani utau*

---

a river in spring
 crossing over the bridge
  a weeping willow

春の川橋を渡れば柳哉
*haru no kawa hashi o watareba yanagi kana*

a bush warbler;
what prompts the young lass from next door to look up?

鶯や隣の娘何故のぞく
*uguisu ya tonari no musume naze nozoku*

so like Girls' Day dolls
they may be husband and wife
first cherry blossoms

雛に似た夫婦もあらん初櫻
*hina ni nita fūfu mo aran hatsuzakura*

field horsetails
a boat slips by with nary a passenger

土筆人なき舟の流れけり
*tsukuzukushi hito naki fune no nagarekeri*

several young trollops pay an unannounced visit
plum blossoms

女郎共推参なるぞ梅の花
*merō domo suisan naru zo ume no hana*

again on that night the sky was hazy and dark—
Genji at Suma

其夜又朧なりけり須磨の巻
*sono yo mata oboro narikeri Suma no maki*[2]

poppy blossoms
so precise their scattering
how unexpected!

罌粟の花左様に散るは慮外なり
*keshi no hana sayō ni chiru wa ryogai nari*

heat haze shimmering relentlessly o'er the grasses

陽炎の落ちつきかねて草の上
*kagerō no ochitsukikanete kusa no ue*

is poetry's muse an apparition there on misty moonlit nights?

詩神とは朧夜に出る化ものか
*shishin to wa oboroyo ni deru bakemono ka*

dawn dreams, I think
  how indistinct

曉の夢かとぞ思ふ朧哉
*akatsuki no yume ka to zo omou oboro kana*

---

standing beside the drying nets
  a gossamer piscine odor

干網に立つ陽炎の腥き
*hoshiami ni tatsu kagerō no namagusaki*

---

on this embankment
  robbed
    first cherry blossoms

此土手で追ひ剥がれしか初櫻
*kono dote de oihagareshika hatsuzakura*

---

trash heap;
  as if mixed in
    plum blossom shadows

掃溜や錯落として梅の影
*hakidame ya sakuraku toshite ume no kage*

SPRING

an undecorated *koto's* pure strains
　　draped across the window
　　　　plum blossom shadows

素琴あり窓に横ふ梅の影
*sokin ari mado ni yokotau ume no kage*

———

a red-blossomed plum
　　*green-leaf,* that flute of yore
　　　　comes unbidden to mind

紅梅に青葉の笛を畫かばや
*kōbai ni aoba no fue o egakaba ya*[3]

———

by a red-blossomed plum waft plaintive zither strains
　　had I a wife

紅梅にあはれ琴ひく妹もがな
*kōbai ni aware koto hiku imo mo gana*

———

an unearthed roof tile at Kokunbuji Temple
　　a cherry tree

國分寺の瓦掘出す櫻かな
*Kokubuji no kawara horidasu sakura kana*

*17*

a cornerstone fragment
    a dawn cherry tree scattering its blossoms

断礎一片有明櫻ちりかゝる
*danso ippen ariakezakura chirikakaru*

---

grilling sardines at an old temple
    spring evening

古寺に鰯燒くなり春の宵
*furudera ni iwashi yakunari haru no yoi*

---

this place of exile
    drying nets in profusion
        the vernal moon

配所には干網多し春の月
*haisho ni wa hoshiami ōshi haru no tsuki*

---

how lamentable;
    to have been born male
        the vernal moon

口惜しや男と生れ春の月
*kuchioshi ya otoko to umare haru no tsuki*

if you listen well, you'll hear a pond snail crying
    inside the pot

よく聞けば田螺鳴くなり鍋の中
*yoku kikeba tanishi nakunari nabe no naku*

in a mountain rose
    unseen by village children
        a pond snail

山吹に里の子見えぬ田螺かな
*yamabuki ni sato no ko mienu tanishi kana*

spring snow on a vermillion tray
    regrets

春の雪朱盆に載せて惜しまるゝ
*haru no yuki shubon ni nosete oshimaruru*

## In the style of the Taoist immortals

I.
on a spring evening I can hear a *biwa*—
  shrine to an angel

春の夜の琵琶聞えけり天女の祠
*haru no yo no biwa kikoekeri tennyo no shi*

II.
the roof ridge;
  the spring wind moans
    a white-fletched arrow

屋の棟や春風鳴つて白羽の矢
*ya no mune ya shunpū natte shiraha no ya*

III.
up rise the mists
  the vermillion bridge vanishes

霞たつて朱ぬりの橋の消にけり
*kasumi tatte shunuri no hashi no kienikeri*

# SPRING

IV.
whence comes that calling of my name?
 the mountains in spring

どこやらで我名よぶなり春の山
*dokoyarade waga na yobunari haru no yama*

V.
the wide heavens;
 from within the mists
 a war whoop

大空や霞の中の鯨波の聲
*ōzora ya kasumi no naka no toki no koe*

VI.
dwelling place of gods
 the spring mountains belch forth white clouds

神の住む春山白き雲を吐く
*kami no sumu haruyama shiroki kumo o haku*

## SŌSEKI NATSUME'S COLLECTED HAIKU

through many mountains to peter out on the plains
   the winds of springtime

乱山の盡きて原なり春の風
*ranzan no tsukite hara nari haru no kaze*

---

fresh, spring grass;
   water drips from a basket of tiny clams

若草や水の滴たる蜆籠
*wakakusa ya mizu no shitataru shijimikago*

---

the moon has set
   plum blossoms by pallid lamplight before the altar

月落ちて佛燈靑し梅の花
*tsuki ochite buttō aoshi ume no hana*

---

spring evening
   a roadside raconteur spinning yarns late into the night

春の夜を辻講釋にふかしける
*haru no yo o tsujikōshaku ni fukashikeru*

*22*

pigeon shit
　　white on a votive tablet on a spring evening

鳩の糞春の夕の絵馬白し
*hato no fun haru no yūbe no ema shiroshi*

a fortune
　　what if it were *your* fate?
　　　　hazy spring moon

辻占のもし君ならば朧月
*tsujiura no moshi kimi naraba oborozuki*

composing poems by the light of an exquisite lamp
　　springtime bitterness

蘭燈に詩をかく春の恨み哉
*rantō ni shi o kaku haru no urami kana*

how ghastly;
　　writing out sutras in blood under a hazy spring moon

恐ろしや經を血でかく朧月
*osoroshi ya kyō o chi de kaku oborozuki*

a cat
   unaware it is a temple pet
      on the prowl for love

猫知らず寺に飼はれて戀わたる
*neko shirazu tera ni kawarete koiwataru*

heat shimmering air
   a crab bubbling as it breaths
      the beach at ebb tide

陽炎に蟹の泡ふく干潟かな
*kagero ni kani no awa fuku higata kana*

an old gourd hanging from the pillar
   wasps have built a nest

古瓢柱に懸けて蜂巣くふ
*furufukube hashira ni kakete hachi sukū*

two appear as one!
   butterflies in flight

二つかと見れば一つに飛ぶや蝶
*futatsu ka to mireba hitotsu ni tobu ya chō*

the first butterfly;
    with no colza blossoms about
      how sad it must be

初蝶や菜の花なくて淋しかろ
*hatsuchō ya nanohana nakute samishikaro*

a dripping well sweep
    scattered plum blossoms
      moonlit night

桔槹切れて梅ちる月夜哉
*hanetsurube kirete ume chiru tsukiyo kana*

cries of a pheasant
    resounding across Ōtakehara Plain

雉子の聲大竹原を鳴り渡る
*kiji no koe Ōtakehara o nariwataru*

welling out of the sand
    spring waters

むくむくと砂の中より春の水
*mukumuku to suna no naka yori haru no mizu*

gilt folding screen rent in myriad places
　　cats in heat

金屏を幾所かきさく猫の戀
*kinbyō o ikusho kakisaku neko no koi*

---

on one knee, he draws his sword
　　the swallow deftly evades the blade

居合抜けば燕ひらりと身をかはす
*iai nukeba tsubame hirari to mi o kawasu*

---

in their midst
　　a shrine of unvarnished wood;
　　　　plum blossoms

其中に白木の宮や梅の花
*sono naka ni shiraki no miya ya ume no hana*

---

sleeping octopus
　　the spring tides have ebbed
　　　　there, between the rocks

章魚眠る春潮落ちて岩の間
*tako nemuru shunchō ochite iwao no ma*

mountain ascetics lined up at the checkpoint;
    plum blossoms

山伏の並ぶ關所や梅の花
*yamabushi no narabu sekisho ya ume no hana*[4]

plum blossoms scatter;
    a waterwheel turns on a moonlit night

梅ちるや月夜に廻る水車
*ume chiru ya tsukiyo ni mawaru mizuguruma*

sobering up
    white plum blossoms on a night clear and cold

酒醒て梅白き夜の冴返る
*sake samete ume shiroki yo no saekaeru*

losing to a crab
    ocellated octopus with but five legs

蟹に負けて飯蛸の足五本なり
*kani ni makete iidako no ashi go hon nari*

on a mountain lane
spooking at plum blossoms
horseback riding

山路來て梅にすくまる馬上哉
*yamaji kite ume ni sukumaru bajō kana*

the dog departs
abruptly
dandelions rebound

犬去つてむつくと起る蒲公英が
*inu satte mukku to okiru tanpopo ga*

on the third day, rain
on the fourth, plum blossoms bloom
my diary

三日雨四日梅咲く日誌かな
*mikka ame yokka ume saku nisshi kana*

in the colza blossoms
    casually taking a dump
        cripes! a courier

菜の花の中に糞ひる飛脚哉
*nanohana no naka ni kuso hiru hikyaku kana*

---

colza blossoms;
    before the gate a young bonze reads out his sutras

菜の花や門前の小僧經を讀む
*nanohana ya monzen no kozō kyō o yomu*[5]

---

though I can see the sea, very far in the distance
    here! a field of colza

海見ゆれど中々長き菜畑哉
*umi miyuredo nakanaka nagaki nabata kana*

---

right above the straw-woven sail it cries;
    soaring skylark

莚帆の眞上に鳴くや揚雲雀
*mushiroho no maue ni naku ya agehibari*

## SŌSEKI NATSUME'S COLLECTED HAIKU

atop a balloon it alights, looking
    skylark

風船にとまりて見たる雲雀哉
*fūsen ni tomarite mitaru hibari kana*

the rain clears
    the southern mountains belch forth spring clouds

雨晴れて南山春の雲を吐く
*ame harete nanzan haru no kumo o haku*

a solitary flock;
    towards northern Noto
        geese heading home

一群や北能州へ帰る雁
*ichigun ya kita Nōshū e kaeru kari*

though the nightingales have departed
    yet, my penury remains

鶯の去れども貧にやつれけり
*uguisu no saredomo hin ni yatsurekeri*

*30*

nightingale;
    in a rice paddy
        a red shrine gate

鶯や田圃の中の赤鳥居
*uguisu ya tanbo no naka no aka torii*

---

the nightingales' cries yet again fill my ears
    midday meal

鶯をまた聞きまする晝餉哉
*uguisu o mata kikimasuru hiruge kana*

---

waxing crescent moon;
    the fields are burning toward the untouchables' village

三日月や野は穢多村へ燒て行く
*mikazuki ya no wa etamura e yaite yuku*

---

ancient road;
    the smell of a swidden
        a bamboo hat in rain

舊道や燒野の匂ひ笠の雨
*kyūdō ya yakeno no nioi kasa no ame*

on field and mountain
  fires are rising
    a pheasant's cry

野に山に焼き立てられて雉の聲
*no ni yama ni yakitaterarete kiji no koe*

swaling the field;
  a scorched milestone on the lands of the State

野を焼くや道標焦る官有地
*no o yaku ya dōhyō kogeru kan'yūchi*

a bamboo grass hedge partitions a swidden

篠竹の垣を隔てゝ焼野哉
*shinodake no kaki o hedatete yakeno kana*

the rattan screen wavers
  someone's silhouette
    perhaps watching butterflies

御簾搖れて蝶御覽ずらん人の影
*misu yurete chō goranzuran hito no kage*

stagnant vermillion water in an inkstone
    a butterfly slakes its thirst

蝶舐る朱硯の水澱みたり
*chō namuru shusuzuri no mizu yodomitari*

---

a storehouse
    red-blossomed plum branches against a black wall

藏つきたり紅梅の枝黒い塀
*kura tsukitari kōbai no eda kuroi hei*

---

seven mountain miles!
    viewing cherry blossoms while wearing high
        wooden clogs

山三里櫻に足駄穿きながら
*yama sanri sakura ni ashida hakinagara*

I long to accompany them on their return
 the geese have all left

連立て歸うと雁皆去りぬ
*tsuretatte karō to kari mina sarinu*

---

grinding her teeth
 the housemaid is quite frightening;
  spring evening

齒ぎしりの下婢恐ろしや春の宵
*hagishiri no kahi osoroshi ya haru no yoi*

---

shaken out of slumber by my wife
 springtime shower

吾妹子に搖り起されつ春の雨
*wagimoko ni yuriokosaretsu haru no ame*

---

a dog flees into Fukadera Temple;
 plum blossoms in spring

普化寺に犬逃げ込むや梅の花
*Fukadera ni inu nigekomu ya ume no hana*

# SPRING

after an overnight tryst a bell sounds
　　how heartlessly cold

きぬぎぬの鐘につれなく冴え返る
*kinuginu no kane ni tsurenaku saekaeru*

---

spring clouds leaving the mountain peaks flow on

春の雲峯をはなれて流れけり
*haru no kumo mine o hanarete nagarekeri*

---

atop the hat of the lead mountain ascetic;
　　camellia petals

先達の斗巾の上や落椿
*sendatsu no tokin no ue ya ochitsubaki*

---

spinning 'round and 'round like Sakata Kinpira
　　a kite

金平のくるりくるりと鳳巾
*Kinpira no kururikururi to ikanobori*[6]

a light coracle wrinkling the water
   the reeds' spring shoots

舟輕し水皺よつて蘆の角
*fune karushi mizushiwa yotte ashi no tsuno*

sprawled on the ground looking up
   cherry blossom viewing in a bamboo basket hat

仰向て深編笠の花見哉
*aomuite fukaamigasa no hanami kana*

a feminine mendicant monk
   mountain cherry blossoms

女らしき虚無僧見たり山櫻
*onna rashiki komusō mitari yamazakura*

o'er the spring estuary, in the far distance
   a temple pagoda

春の江の開いて遠し寺の塔
*haru no e no hiraite tōshi tera no tō*

SPRING

a willow weeps
    the river flows on to the south

柳垂れて江は南に流れけり
*yanagi tarete e wa minami ni nagarekeri*

across the river bloom cherry blossoms—
    imadoyaki pottery

川向ひ櫻咲きけり今土燒
*kawa mukai sakura sakikeri imadoyaki*[7]

dampened by the rain
    there is nowhere the nightingales aren't calling

雨に濡れて鶯鳴かぬ處なし
*ame ni nurete uguisu nakanu tokoro nashi*

the mist obscures the towering pine trees
    provincial border

霞むのは高い松なり國境
*kasumu no wa takai matsu nari kunizakai*

the bamboo blind moves
  a person there, yes or no?
    flittering butterfly

御簾搖れて人ありや否や飛ぶ胡蝶
*misu yurete hito ari yainya tobu kochō*

topping the clouds
  up soars Ryōunkaku tower
    lost in the mist

登りたる凌雲閣の霞かな
*noboritaru Ryōunkaku kasumi kana*[8]

bamboo trees in languid undulation—
  a mountain in spring

糢糊として竹動きけり春の山
*moko toshite take ugokikeri haru no yama*

antiquated Edo-era woodblock print;
  vernal rain shower

古ぼけた江戸錦繪や春の雨
*furuboketa Edo nishikie ya haru no ame*

curse the haze!
　　I know not her heart or my way
　　　　to love

朧故に行衛も知らぬ戀をする
*oboro yue ni yukue mo shiranu koi o suru*[9]

setting the weak-legged astride a steed
　　mountain cherry blossoms

足弱を馬に乘せたり山櫻
*ashiyowa o uma ni nosetari yamazakura*

**Lamenting Kohaku on the one-year anniversary**

you don't return
　　where have you travelled to see the flowers?

君歸らず何處の花を見にいたか
*kimi kaerazu izuko no hana o mini ita ka*

long day;
    he leaves to me the yawning
        as he departs

永き日や欠伸うつして別れ行く
*nagaki hi ya akubi utsushite wakareyuku*

---

**Entrusted to Kyoshi to give to Seigetsu when I departed Matsuyama for Kumamoto**

to depart without meeting
    you know I shall water the flowers with my tears

逢はで去る花に涙を濺げかし
*awade saru hana ni namida o sosogekashi*[10]

---

there in the city
    one of your pets
        a croaking frog

市中に君に飼はれて鳴く蛙
*ichinaka ni kimi ni kawarete naku kaeru*

## Love's Parting

I see you off;
   quietly laps the brimming spring tide of tears

見送るや春の潮のひたひたに
*miokuru ya haru no ushio no hitahita ni*

## Interrupted Love

has she forgotten?
   she feigns ignorance tilling a field

忘れしか知らぬ顔して畠打つ
*wasureshika shiranu kao shite hatake utsu*

## Frustrated Love

of spring's departure
   strumming a *koto*
      bungling the strains

行春を琴掻き鳴らし掻き亂す
*yuku haru o koto kakinarashi kakimidasu*

## Dead Love

my heart turned to stone
yet I remain unconcerned
hazy moon

化石して強面なくならう朧月
*kasekishite tsurenaku narō oborozuki*

---

around the boulder shallow water flows
alas! spring is yet far off

岩を廻る水に淺きを恨む春
*iwa o mawaru mizu ni asaki o uramu haru*

---

died a human
reborn a crane
clear and cold

人に死し鶴に生れて冴返る
*hito ni shishi tsuru ni umarete saekaeru*

SPRING

when the vernal east wind blows one will doubtless catch cold
    lightly clad

恐らくば東風に風ひくべき薄着
*osorakuba kochi ni kaze hiku beki usugi*

was it Hanshan?
    was it Shide?
        stung by a wasp

寒山か拾得か蜂に螫されしは
*Kanzan ka Jittoku ka hachi ni sasareshi wa*[11]

drooping atop a horsefly
    the camellia

落ちさまに虻を伏せたる椿哉
*ochisama ni abu o fusetaru tsubaki kana*

coming to a mountain temple rife with stray cats
    I fell in love

のら猫の山寺に来て戀をしつ
*noraneko no yamadera ni kite koi o shitsu*

flag of the imperial troops;
   through the mists travels a cart

大纛や霞の中を行く車
*daitō ya kasumi no naka o yuku kuruma*

---

willows
   a river
      as if I were in a *nanga* painting

柳あり江あり南畫に似たる吾
*yanagi ari e ari nanga ni nitaru ware*[12]

---

well-aged vinegar
   the three sages grimace
      peach blossoms

醋熟して三聖顰す桃の花
*su jukushite sansei hinsu momo no hana*[13]

across the river
here and there cows
veiled in mist

川を隔て散點す牛霞みけり
*kawa o hedate santensu ushi kasumikeri*

---

that fragrance is a perfume called Imperial Court;
spring

薫ずるは大内といふ香や春
*kunzuru wa ōuchi to iu kō ya haru*

---

a worthy opponent!
to whom belongs that plum-marked battle banner?

よき敵ぞ梅の指物するは誰
*yoki teki zo ume no sashimono suru wa dare*

---

hazy moonlit night;
perchance there is love for unusual faces too

朧夜や顔に似合ぬ戀もあらん
*oboroyo ya kao ni niawanu koi mo aran*

atop the mountain
    the enemy's red flag
        veiled in mist

山の上に敵の赤旗霞みけり
*yama no ue ni teki no akahata kasumikeri*[14]

---

the quinces are blooming;
    I must strive to live taking the long view

木瓜咲くや漱石拙を守るべく
*boke saku ya Sōseki setsu o mamorubeku*

---

a spring evening
    Kenkō must have felt some rancor in his black priestly garb

春の夜を兼好緇衣に恨
*haru no yo o Kenkō shii ni urami ari*[15]

---

taking advantage of the warmth
    I annihilate all the lice at one go

暖に乗じ一挙蝨をみなごろしにす
*dan ni jōji ikkyo shirami o minagoroshi ni su*

how I wish to be reborn as inconspicuous as a violet

菫程な小さき人に生
*sumire hodo na chiisaki hito ni umaretashi*

reflected in the water
  purple wisteria against scarlet carp

水に映る藤紫に鯉緋なり
*mizu ni utsuru fuji murasaki ni koi hi nari*

**Characters**

the character 'ha—*tomoe*' is harder than 'i—well'—
  plum blossoms

いの字よりはの字むつかし梅の花
*i no ji yori ha no ji mutsukashi ume no hana*

## Characters

in gold paint
copying out the Lotus Sutra
what a long day

金泥もて法華經寫す日永哉
*kindei mote hokkekyō utsusu hinaga kana*

## Chanting

a spring evening
the chanting of Nō solos fills a house

春の夜を小謠はやる家中哉
*haru no yo o kōtai hayaru kachū kana*

mid-afternoon
grubbing in a spacious field
a lone figure

八時の廣き畑打つ一人かな
*yatsudoki no hiroki hata utsu hitori kana*

dropping their horns and tilting their necks
    the deer of Nara

角落ちて首傾けて奈良の鹿
*tsuno ochite kubi katamukete Nara no shika*

huge amidst the colza blossoms
    the setting sun

菜の花の中へ大きな入日かな
*nanohana no naka e ōkina irihi kana*

spring breezes through myriad windows
    a vernal stream through the gate

夥し窓春の風門春の水
*Oobitadashi mado haru no kaze mon haru no mizu*

in a quagmire how much quieter it is
    the departure of spring

泥海の猶しづかなり春の暮
*nukarumi no nao shizukanari haru no kure*

lushly enclosed by pines
 cherry blossoms in the valley

松をもて圍ひし谷の櫻かな
*matsu o mote kakoishi tani no sakura kana*

cherry trees soaked by rain and clouds
 in the mountains' shadow

雨に雲に櫻濡れたり山の陰
*ame ni kumo ni sakura nuretari yama no kage*

amid dampened blossoms
 people without umbrellas
  a cold rain

花に濡るゝ傘なき人の雨を寒み
*hana ni nururu kasa naki hito no ame o sami*

encountering no one
 a profusion of blossoms in the rainy mountains

人に逢はず雨ふる山の花盛
*hito ni awazu ame furu yama no hanazakari*

SPRING

the high mountains
   capriciously comes spring cloud cover

山高し動ともすれば春曇る
*yama takashi yaya to mo sureba haru kumoru*

delicately the late March clouds float by

濃かに彌生の雲の流れけり
*komayaka ni yayoi no kumo no nagarekeri*

changing out the gold brocade hanging scroll
   a vernal breeze

金襴の軸懸け替て春の風
*kinran no jiku kakekaete haru no kaze*

colza seeds bloom
   a shallow river embraces an eyot

菜種咲く小島を抱いて淺き川
*natane saku kojima o daite asaki kawa*

a willow tree
    drooping over a white duck

柳ありて白き家鴨に枝垂たり
*yanagi arite shiroki ahiru ni shidaretari*

---

the passing of spring
    paleness after shaving off eyebrows

行く春を剃り落したる眉青し
*yuku haru o soriotoshitaru mayu aoshi*

---

a spring evening;
    the sound of robes as a lady-in-waiting departs

春の夜や局をさがる衣の音
*haru no yo ya tsubone o sagaru kinu no oto*

---

fallen plum blossoms never fail to move me
    new *haiku*

梅ちつてそゞろなつかしむ新俳句
*ume chitte sozoro natsukashimu shinhaiku*[16]

SPRING

the hanging calabash rattles
   spring winds

瓢かけてからからと鳴る春の風
*fukube kakete karakara to naru haru no kaze*

---

hanging a birdcage in a willow tree
   a cozy garden

鳥籠を柳にかけて狭き庭
*torikago o yanagi ni kakete semaki niwa*

---

meeting on Sanjō Bridge
   hazy spring moon

三條の上で逢ひけり朧月
*sanjō no ue de aikeri oborozuki*

---

spilling onto a *koto* set to the side
   hazy spring moonlight

片寄する琴に落ちけり朧月
*katayosuru koto ni ochikeri oborozuki*

a back gate;
    lowering the drawbridge in the hazy spring moonlight

搦手やはね橋下す朧月
*karamete ya hanebashi orosu oborozuki*

the splash of night fishing nets suddenly cast;
    a spring river

颯と打つ夜網の音や春の川
*satto utsu yoami no oto ya haru no kawa*

spring night
    a student blowing a grass whistle

春の夜のしば笛を吹く書生哉
*haru no yo no shibabue o fuku shosei kana*

cranes loosed in the shrine grounds—
    plum blossoms

神苑に鶴放ちけり梅の花
*shin'en ni tsuru hanachikeri ume no hana*

SPRING

a mistress and man
  the weeping willow tells of their parting

妾と郎離別を語る柳哉
*shō to rō ribetsu o kataru yanagi kana*

waiting for her young man
  a weeping willow at their trysting place

郎を待つ待合茶屋の柳かな
*rō o matsu machiaijaya no yanagi kana*

cracking a whip
  the cattle remain immobile as the day drags on

鞭つて牛動かざる日永かな
*muchiutte ushi ugokazaru hinaga kana*

worldly desires so like the moonlit haze
  such a night

煩悩の朧に似たる夜もありき
*bonnō no oboro ni nitaru yo mo ariki*

now and again I imagine dying
   hazy night

吾折々死なんと思ふ朧かな
*ware oriori shinan to omou oboro kana*

---

## 40 [of 105] poems on plum blossoms

impoverished, Confucius took thin rice gruel in his study
   plum blossoms all around

夫子貧に梅花書屋の粥薄し
*Fūshi hin ni baika shooku no kayu usushi*

---

tailing the horse's rump, we descend;
   plum trees on a steep path

馬の尻に尾して下るや岨の梅
*uma no shiri ni bishite kudaru ya sowa no ume*

---

that smell of plum blossoms and *sake*-lees pickles
   takes me back

奈良漬に梅に其香をなつかしむ
*narazuke ni ume ni sono ka o natsukashimu*

white smoke from a night train
    plum blossoms in my mind's eye

夜汽車より白きを梅と推しけり
*yogisha yori shiroki o ume to suishikeri*

---

only the nameless dead now dwell here
    plum blossoms

死して名なき人のみ住んで梅の花
*shishite na naki hito nomi sunde ume no hana*

---

telling tales of Gyokuran and Taiga
    plum blossoms

玉蘭と大雅と語る梅の花
*Gyokuran to Taiga to kataru ume no hana*[17]

---

selling incense pastilles in a plum bedecked alley
    an old man

梅の小路練香ひさぐ翁かな
*ume no kōji nerikō hisagu okina kana*

in a jasper bowl
  a fallen plum blossom

碧玉の茶碗に梅の落花かな
*hekigyoku no chawan ni ume no rakka kana*

in the sunlight;
  the owner of plum trees wipes clean a sword

日當りや刀を拭ふ梅の主
*hiatari ya katana o nuguu ume no nushi*

awaking early
  sipping miso soup;
    a plum tree next door

とく起て味噌する梅の隣かな
*toku okite miso suru ume no tonari kana*

atop a bamboo dowsing rod
   plum blossoms falling
      before the main shrine

筮竹に梅ちりかゝる社頭哉
*zeichiku ni ume chirikakaru shatō kana*

---

wordlessly a young child points
   distant plum trees

ものいはず童子遠くの梅を指す
*mono iwazu dōji tōku no ume o sasu*

moonlight
white plum blossoms in the village at the mountain's foot

月に望む麓の村の梅白し
*tsuki ni nozomu fumoto no mura no ume shiroshi*

fallen plum blossoms
borne along the millrace to the waterwheel

落梅花水車の門を流れけり
*rakubaika suisha no mon o nagarekeri no hana*

splitting wood under a plum tree
an old man's jaundiced face

梅の下に槇割る翁の面黄也
*ume no shita ni maki waru ō no omo ki nari*

by a plum tree at daybreak flows a gurgling stream

曉の梅に下りて嗽ぐ
*akatsuki no ume ni kudarite kuchisusugu*

SPRING

with a cry the crane took wing
  plums in the darkness

戛と鳴て鶴飛び去りぬ闇の梅
*katsu to naite tsuru tobisarinu yami no ume*

the sneeze of a sleepless monk;
  midnight plum blossoms

眠らざる僧の嚔や夜半の梅
*nemurazaru sō no kusame ya yowa no ume*

sparsely arranged in an old copper vase
  plum blossoms

古銅瓶に疎らな梅を活けてけり
*kodōhei ni mabarana ume o iketekeri*

fragrant India ink;
  the "old plum grove" in the ancient capital Nara

墨の香や奈良の都の古梅園
*sumi no ka ya Nara no miyako no kobaien*[18]

a temple festival
the plums bloom disquieted by the throngs

縁日の梅窮屈に咲きにけり
*ennichi no ume kyūkutsu ni sakinikeri*

---

neither lighting a lamp nor closing the storm shutters
plums blossoms

灯もつけず雨戸も引かず梅の花
*hi mo tsukezu amado mo hikazu ume no hana*

---

a Tokyo-bound steam engine departs Hakone
white plum blossoms

上り汽車の箱根を出て梅白し
*nobori kisha no Hakone o idete ume shiroshi*

---

painting an angular plum tree;
Shunsei

佶倔な梅を畫くや謝春星
*kikkutsuna ume o egaku ya sha Shunsei*[19]

SPRING

inching up the privy wall;
    plum tree shadow

雪隠の壁に上るや梅の影
*setsuin no kabe ni noboru ya ume no kage*

———

a temple rich with plum trees
    the chatter of folks at the mountain's foot

梅の寺麓の人語聞こゆなり
*ume no tera fumoto no jingo kikoyu nari*

———

the pure face of the head priest of the shrine;
    plum blossoms

清げなる宮司の面や梅の花
*kiyoge naru gūji no tsura ya ume no hana*

———

the moon rises
    plum blossom shadows fall upon my pillow

月升つて枕に落ちぬ梅の影
*tsuki nobotte makura ni ochinu ume no kage*

hearing a Kyoto lilt ask of crimson plum blossoms
  I paid the city a visit

京音の紅梅ありやと尋ねけり
*kyōon no kōbai ari ya to tazunekeri*


crimson plum blossoms;
  an old house with resident ghosts

紅梅や物の化の住む古館
*kōbai ya mononoke no sumu furuyakata*


crimson plum blossoms
  a poem recited by a paramour

梅紅ひめかけの歌に咏まれけり
*ume kurenai mekake no uta ni yomarekeri*


in a plum grove on the verge of blooming
  two or three blossoms

藪の梅危く咲きぬ二三輪
*yabu no ume ayauku sakinu ni-sanrin*

# SPRING

a susurrous stream tucked between ancient plum trees

潺湲の水挾む古梅かな
*senkan no mizu sashihasamu kobai kana*

---

early plum blossoms striking a chevron gong
　　Gekkeiji Temple

寒梅に磬を打つなり月桂寺
*kanbai ni kei o utsu nari Gekkeiji*

---

rambling hither and yon through the plum trees
　　yesterday
　　　　today

梅遠近そゞろあるきす昨日今日
*ume ochikochi sozoro arukisu kinō kyō*

---

the moon rises
　　to wander once again among the plum trees

月升つて再び梅に徘徊す
*tsuki nobotte futatabi ume ni haikaisu*

a hoary trunk;
    the morning star shines upon the learnèd hermit's plum

鐵幹や曉星を點ず居士の梅
*tekkan ya gyōsei o tenzu koji no ume*

---

*koto* strings vibrate pleasingly with each ax blow;
    plum blossoms

琴に打つ斧の響や梅の花
*koto ni utsu ono no hibiki ya ume no hana*

---

the spirit of a plum is a beautiful woman
    the spirit of a pine is an old man

梅の精は美人にて松の精は翁也
*ume no sei wa bijin nite matsu no sei wa okina nari*

---

a single early blossom called "plum in snow"

一輪を雪中梅と名けけり
*ichirin o setchūbai to nazukekeri*

the resonant tolling of a bell—
    spring's eventide

ごんと鳴る鐘をつきけり春の暮
*gon to naru kane o tsukikeri haru no kure*

it first seems a white butterfly
    ah! but it's a yellow one

白き蝶をふと見染めけり黄なる蝶
*shiroki chō o futo misomekeri ki naru chō*

fold upon fold of purple drapes;
    mountains famed for cherry blossoms

紫の幕をた〻むや花の山
*murasaki no maku o tatamu ya hana no yama*

whether priest or layman
    quince blossoms when they enter the hermitage

僧か俗か庵を這入れば木瓜の花
*sō ka zoku ka iori o haireba boke no hana*

a town of many temples;
  quince blossoms in the earthen wall cracks

寺町や土塀の隙の木瓜の花
*teramachi ya dobei no suki no boke no hana*

nightingales and willows, too
  this dwelling in verdure

鶯も柳も靑き住居かな
*uguisu mo yanagi mo aoki sumai kana*

stretched out atop fresh tatami mats
  spring evening

新しき畳に寐たり宵の春
*atarashiki tatami ni netari yoi no haru*

spring rain
  lugging pots and pans

春の雨鍋と釜とを運びけり
*haru no ame nabe to kama to o hakobikeri*

SPRING

my wife appears in a spring-night dream!
    it has come to that

吾妹子を夢みる春の夜となりぬ
*wagimoko o yume miru haru no yo to narinu*

violets discovered;
    lingering light of evening

見付たる菫の花や夕明り
*mitsuketaru sumire no hana ya yūakari*[20]

painting spring overhead;
    castles in the sky

人の上春を寫すや繪そら言
*hito no ue haru o utsusu ya esoragoto*

sleeping snuggled together
    spring rain

寄りそへばねむりておはす春の雨
*yorisoeba nemuriteowasu haru no ame*

## From *Kusamakura* 4 [of 17] poems

spring breeze;
    the sound of horse bells in Izen's ears

春風や惟然が耳に馬の鈴
*harukaze ya Izen ga mimi ni uma no suzu*[21]

———

enticing down the stars of spring
    a midnight garland in her hair

春の星を落して夜半のかざしかな
*haru no hoshi o otoshite yowa no kazashi kana*

———

spring draws resolutely to its close
    I am alone

思ひ切つて更け行く春の獨りかな
*omoikitte fukeyuku haru no hitori kana*

———

I stare at the sky and see naught but magnolia blossoms

木蓮の花許りなる空を瞻る
*mokuren no hana bakari naru sora o miru*

a house of pleasure;
 through the gaps in the balustrade
  the spring ocean

靑樓や欄のひまより春の海
*seirō ya ran no hima yori haru no umi*

spring rain;
 arriving at the public bath with dampened toe covers

春雨や爪革濡るゝ湯屋迄
*harusame ya tsumakawa nururu yūya made*

an untilled field
 myriad crisscrossing shadows of small birds

打つ畠に小鳥の影の屢す
*utsu hata ni kotori no kage no shibashiba su*

on a chilly trip
 Kyoto in a drizzling spring rain

旅に寒し春を時雨れの京にして
*tabi ni samushi haru o shigure no kyō ni shite*

only the eyes of a tomcat in rut loom large
  the rest is scrawny

戀猫の眼ばかりに瘠せにけり
*koineko no manako bakari ni yasenikeri*

---

**Felicitations to Nomura Denshi on his Marriage**

treading daily through fragrant grasses;
  a couple together

日毎踏む草芳しや二人連
*higoto fumu kusakōbashi ya futarizure*[22]

---

green willow
  drooping down above an ornamental post cap

靑柳擬寶珠の上に垂るゝなり
*aoyanagi giboshi no ue ni taruru nari*

---

a person standing at the gate performing for *sake*;
  flowers in his hat

門に立てば酒乞ふ人や帽に花
*kado ni tateba sake kou hito ya mō ni hana*

SPRING

an arrangement of ocellate octopus;
　　indigo plate

飯蛸の一かたまりや皿の藍
*iidako no hito katamari ya sara no ai*

hazy weather as the cherries bloom
　　the sound of the mountain-top bell

花曇り尾上の鐘の響かな
*hanagumori onoe no kane no hibiki kana*[23]

scattered by the attendant's wicker pack
　　cherry blossoms

強力の笈に散る櫻かな
*gōriki no oibako ni chiru sakura kana*

on the nandina
　　a feather's weight;
　　　　spring snow

南天に寸の重みや春の雪
*nanten ni sun no omomi ya haru no yuki*

a temptress' eyebrows;
    early spring

そゝのかす女の眉や春淺し
*sosonokasu onna no mayu ya haru asashi*

———

perforated coins in my kimono sleeve;
    the twilight of spring

穴のある錢が袂に暮の春
*ana no aru zeni ga tamoto ni kure no haru*

———

spring departs;
    a hanging gourd tells the prioress is away

逝く春や庵主の留守の懸瓢
*yuku haru ya anshu no rusu no kakefukube*

———

**Spring scenery at my home**

a single late-blooming cherry
    how poignant

おくれたる一本櫻憐なり
*okuretaru ipponzakura aware nari*

SPRING

a faint hint of spring
    in the capital poetry flows more fluidly

春はもの〻句になり易し京の町
*haru wa monono ku ni nari yasushi kyō no machi*

---

to the temple
    over two miles through the mist

御堂まで一里あまりの霞かな
*godō made ichiri amari no kasumi kana*

the butterfly has flown
the kitten crouches once more

蝶去つてまた蹲踞る小猫かな
*chō satte mata uzukumaru koneko kana*

neither dolls nor horses move—
tranquility

人形も馬もうごかぬ長閑さよ
*ningyō mo uma mo ugokanu nodokesa yo*

a small whirlpool at the bridge piling;
spring river

橋杭に小さき渦や春の川
*hashigui ni chiisaki uzu ya haru no kawa*

three times over the same bridge
spring night

同じ橋三たび渡りぬ春の宵
*onaji hashi mitabi watarinu haru no yoi*

SPRING

two or three camellias in a tranquil garden
　　the hint of a spring day

茶の木二三本閑庭にちよと春日哉
*chanoki ni-sanbon kantei ni choto harubi kana*

a long day
　　alone with peaceful thoughts

日は永し一人居に静かなる思ひ
*hi wa nagashi hitorii ni shizuka naru omoi*

incense ash white where it fell
　　a long day

線香のこぼれて白き日永哉
*senkō no koborete shiroki hinaga kana*

alone I sleep under a pine tree
　　a long day

我一人松下に寐たる日永哉
*ware hitori shōka ni netaru hinaga kana*

a snagged rubber balloon;
willow tree

引かゝる護謨風船や柳の木
*hikkakaru gomufūsen ya yanagi no ki*

---

a sachet;
how like a trysting tea house in the spring rain

誰袖や待合らしき春の雨
*tagasode ya machiai rashiki haru no ame*

---

on the magnolias
a gentle rain as fleeting as a dream

木蓮に夢の様なる小雨哉
*mokuren ni yume no yō naru kosame kana*

---

imperceptible though the rainfall may be
droplets on flowers

降るとしも見えぬに花の雫哉
*furu to shimo mienu ni hana no shizuku kana*

night drags on;
   asked to remain behind to look after the place

永き日や頼まれて留守居してゐれば
*nagaki hi ya tanomarete rusui shiteireba*

spring chill—
   still a fox-fur overcoat

春寒し未だ狐の裘
*haru samushi imada kitsune no kawagoromo*

a town with many temples;
   peach blossoms through gaps in the hedge

寺町や垣の隙より桃の花
*teramachi ya kaki no suki yori momo no hana*

dyed cloth and willow trees, both ruffled—
   a spring breeze

染物も柳も吹かれ春の風
*somemono mo yanagi mo fukare haru no kaze*

deep within the forsythia;
    the click of playing a *go* stone

連翹の奥や碁を打つ石の音
*rengyō no oku ya go o utsu ishi no oto*

---

cherry viewing under cloudy skies
    snacking on *dango*

花曇り御八つに食ふは団子哉
*hanagumori oyatsu ni kuu wa dango kana*

---

a town with many temples;
    spring snow on the camellia blossoms

寺町や椿の花に春の雪
*teramachi ya tsubaki no hana ni haru no yuki*

---

a lacquered hat
    the distant Kawachi Road shrouded in mist

塗笠に遠き河内路霞みけり
*nurigasa ni tōki Kawachiji kasumikeri*

SPRING

serenity
   the sound of a teakettle in the spring rain

靜かなるは春の雨にて釜の音
*shizukanaru wa haru no ame nite kama no oto*

a visitor comes astride a donkey
   a willow at the gate

驢に騎して客來る門の柳哉
*ro ni kishite kyaku kuru mon no yanagi kana*

greensward;
   a dog's dream as gossamer as the heat shimmer

芝草や陽炎ふひまを犬の夢
*shibakusa ya kagerō hima o inu no yume*

the form of fish in the depths
   time and again
      water in spring

魚の影底にしばしば春の水
*uo no kage soko ni shibashiba haru no mizu*

meditating
　　ears cocked
　　　　the sound of spring rain in the cavernous hall

靜坐聽くは虚堂に春の雨の音
*seiza kiku wa kyodō ni haru no ame no oto*

playing a *koto*
　　watching the falling blossoms

一張の琴鳴らし見る落花哉
*itchō no koto narashi miru rakka kana*

a leisurely game of *go*
　　quietly placing the stones in spring

局に閑あり靜かに下す春の石
*kyoku ni kan ari shizuka ni orosu haru no ishi*

on a silver folding screen
　　the chill of spring plums done in charcoal ink

銀屏に墨もて梅の春寒し
*ginbyō ni sumi mote ume no haru samushi*

*82*

# SPRING

even odds the bamboo shoots end up canned
    early spring

筍は鑵詰ならん淺き春
*takenoko wa kanzume naran asaki haru*

---

the passing of spring;
    whence these whiskers on my cheeks?

行く春や知らざるひまに頬の髭
*yuku haru ya shirazaru hima ni hō no hige*

---

a nightingale now?
    I am getting a shave

鶯や髪剃あてゝ貰ひ居る
*uguisu ya kamisori atete moraiiru*

---

warmed *sake* yet at this date—
    the lingering chill of spring

酒の燗此頃春の寒き哉
*sake no kan konogoro haru no samuki kana*

a young wife's umbrella
    held aslant on the embankment;
        spring winds

嫁の傘傾く土手や春の風
*yome no kasa katamuku dote ya haru no kaze*

---

a home hidden by peach blossoms
    a barking dog

桃の花隠れ家なるに吠ゆる犬
*momo no hana kakureya naru ni hoyuru inu*

---

a tea house;
    an Ashiya teakettle as the end of spring draws nigh

草庵や蘆屋の釜に暮るゝ春
*sōan ya Ashiya no kama ni kururu haru*

---

sagging barge towline;
    swallows

牽船の縄のたるみや乙鳥
*hikibune no nawa no tarumi ya tsubakurame*

SPRING

to think that there's even swallow poop on the bung
wine shop

呑口に乙鳥の糞も酒屋哉
*nomiguchi ni tsubame no fun mo sakaya kana*

drooping over the wall of a restaurant
a willow

料理屋の塀から垂れて柳かな
*ryōriya no hei kara tarete yanagi kana*

the willow buds blowing
a meal at an inn on Shijō Road

柳芽を吹いて四條のはたごかな
*yanagime o fuite Shijō no hatago kana*

## Taking lodging in Kiyamachi and sending this to O-Taka across the river

separated by the river in spring
a man and a young woman

春の川を隔てゝ男女かな
*Haru no kawa o hedatete otoko omina kana*[24]

---

## To Shizue

the young girl has turned ten—
plum blossoms

女の子十になりけり梅の花
*onna no ko tō ni narikeri ume no hana*[25]

---

spraying the white plum blossoms;
a waterwheel

白梅にしぶきかゝるや水車
*hakubai ni shibukikakaru ya mizuguruma*

SPRING

nightingale;
    a lone straw raincoat diving through a thicket

鶯や藪くゞり行く蓑一つ
*uguisu ya yabu kuguriyuku mino hitotsu*


engaging an itinerant minstrel
    spring evening

琵琶法師召されて春の夜なりけり
*biwahōshi mesarete haru no yo narikeri*


spring rain;
    bodies close together under a single umbrella

春雨や身をすり寄せて一つ傘
*harusame ya mi o suriyosete hitotsugasa*


having my ears cleaned
    spring breeze

耳の穴掘つて貰ひぬ春の風
*mimi no ana hottemorainu haru no kaze*

# SŌSEKI NATSUME'S COLLECTED HAIKU

spring rains;
  low-end lodgings on the Shikoku pilgrimage

春雨や四國遍路の木賃宿
*harusame ya Shikoku henro no kichinyado*

# Summer

## 夏

when you make your way home
   cry not, but laugh little cuckoo

歸ろふと泣かずに笑へ時鳥
*kaerō to nakazu ni warae hototogisu*

clouds on the peak drip
   water burbles through a drain pipe

峯の雲落ちて筧に水の音
*mine no kumo ochite kakei ni mizu no oto*

held aloft in the summer rain;
   bull's-eye umbrella

さみだれに持ちあつかふや蛇目傘
*samidare ni mochiatsukau ya janomegasa*

catching fireflies
    ah, but I landed myself in the brook

螢狩われを小川に落としけり
*hotarugari ware o ogawa ni otoshikeri*

---

cooling in the shady grove
    but the mosquitoes!
        I am their dinner

藪陰に涼んで蚊にぞ喰はれける
*yabukage ni suzunde ka ni zo kuwarekeru*

---

refreshing coolness;
    green pine needles on my nappping face

涼しさや晝寐の貌に青松葉
*suzushisa ya hirune no kao ni aomatsuba*

---

oppressive warmth
    cicadas thrum in my afternoon dreams

暑苦し晝寐の夢に蟬の聲
*atsukurushi hirune no yume ni semi no koe*

if you serenade, serenade, then, to the full moon
little cuckoo

鳴くならば満月になけほとゝぎす
*nakunaraba mangetsu ni nake hototogisu*

dark mountains,
bright mountains;
cloud-swathed peaks

暗き山明るき山や雲の峯
*kuraki yama akaruki yama ya kumo no mine*

coolness
a large waterwheel turns

涼しさを大水車廻りけり
*suzushisa o ōmizuguruma mawarikeri*

cool moonlight;
a horseman washing his steed on the river bank

月涼し馬士馬洗ふ河原哉
*tsuki suzushi bashi uma arau kawara kana*

the fragrant cedar at Uragashi
    little cuckoo

裏河岸の杉の香ひや時鳥
*Uragashi no sugi no nioi ya hototogisu*

every Tom, Dick, and Harry lends an ear
    little cuckoo

猫も聞け杓子も是へ時鳥
*neko mo kike shakushi mo kore e hototogisu*

a lake;
    seven miles to the hot spring source
        little cuckoo

湖や湯元へ三里時鳥
*mizuumi ya yumoto e sanri hototogisu*

# SUMMER

early summer rain;
    wherever I might venture
        little cuckoo

五月雨ぞ何處まで行ても時鳥
*samidare zo doko made itte mo hototogisu*

weight loss in these days of summer heat
    even mosquitos don't feed on me

夏瘦の此頃蚊にもせゝられず
*natsuyase no kono goro ka ni mo seserarezu*

thinking this day of my dear departed mother
    seasonal clothing change

亡き母の思はるゝ哉衣がへ
*naki haha no omowaruru kana koromogae*

Japanese snowflowers
    bamboo head-gear quite hidden in their midst

卯の花に深編笠の隠れけり
*unohana ni fukaamigasa no kakurekeri*

dirt and dust
the heat felt by Yan Zi's coachman

塵埃り晏子の御者の暑哉
*chiri hokori anshi no gyosha no atsusa kana*[1]

---

struck
it belches out the noontime mosquitoes
wooden Buddhist gong

叩かれて晝の蚊を吐く木魚哉
*tatakarete hiru no ka o haku mokugyo kana*

---

a wild waterfall;
the whole mountain's young leaves all aquiver

あら瀧や滿山の若葉皆震ふ
*ara taki ya manzan no wakaba mina furuu*

---

with an errant leap a frog comes this way
my paddy boat

踏はづす蛙是へと田舟哉
*fumi hazusu kaeru kore e to tabune kana*

grass-covered mountains;
   carved out in the south
      wheat fields

草山や南をけづり麦畑
*kusayama ya minami o kezuri mugibatake*

---

the tsunami recedes and in its wake, horror;
   May rains

海嘯去つて後すさまじや五月雨
*tsunami satte ato susamaji ya satsuki ame*

---

converging
   scattering
      fireflies over the river

かたまるや散るや螢の川の上
*katamaru ya chiru ya hotaru no kawa no ue*

---

a single one stealthily crosses the room
   firefly

一つすうと座敷を拔る螢かな
*hitotsu sūto zashiki o nukeru hotaru kana*

SŌSEKI NATSUME'S COLLECTED HAIKU

surrounding a monk deep in meditation
　whining mosquito

禪定の僧を圍んで鳴く蚊かな
*zenjō no sō o kakonde naku ka kana*

moving diagonally across a banana leaf;
　a snail

筋違に芭蕉渡るや蝸牛
*sujikai ni bashō wataru ya katatsumuri*

a short summer night's dream
　I lack even the time to recollect it

短夜の夢思ひ出すひまもなし
*mijikayo no yume omoidasu hima mo nashi*

toward the family Buddhist altar I turn my ass
　a round fan

佛壇に尻を向けたる團扇かな
*butsudan ni shiri o muketaru uchiwa kana*

96

SUMMER

impoverishment
   just white paper mosquito nets in my hermitage

貧しさは紙帳ほどなる庵かな
*mazushisa wa shichō hodo naru iori kana*

the midday cannon sounds o'er the local castle;
   cloud-swathed peaks

午砲打つ地城の上や雲の峯
*gohō utsu jishiro no ue ya kumo no mine*

the sound of a bugle from an army on the march;
   cloud-swathed peaks

行軍の喇叭の音や雲の峯
*kōgun no rappa no oto ya kumo no mine*

coming through the refreshing coolness of the dark—
   Suma Bay

涼しさの闇を來るなり須磨の浦
*shizushisa no yami o kurunari Suma no ura*

a guest making a scene at a public bath
   the heat

銭湯に客のいさかふ暑かな
*sentō ni kyaku no isakau atsusa kana*

---

so cool;
   hugging the great temple bell

涼しさや大釣鐘を抱て居る
*suzushisa ya ōtsurigane o daiteiru*

SUMMER

a sudden evening shower pelting into the lake
　what vigor

夕立の湖に落ち込む勢かな
*yūdachi no umi ni ochikomu kioi kana*

I'll not say, "I've aged"
　seasonal clothing change

吾老いぬとは申すまじ更衣
*ware oinu to wa mōsumaji koromogae*

the red brick dwelling of the foreigner;
　hemp-palm blossoms

異人住む赤い煉瓦や棕櫚の花
*ijin sumu akai renga ya shuro no hana*

flagstones;
　100 meters of continuous hemp-palm blossoms

敷石や一丁つゞく棕櫚の花
*shikiishi ya itchō tsuzuku shuro no hana*

a recluse returns home;
    irksome whining mosquito

獨居の歸ればむつと鳴く蚊哉
*hitorii no kaereba mutto naku ka kana*

---

to spend the short summer night with you
    or to accept 2,000 *koku*

短夜を君と寐ようか二千石とらうか
*mijikayo o kimi to neyō ka nisengoku torō ka*[2]

---

love letter;
    turning my sleeves inside out for summer airing

玉章や袖裏返す土用干
*tamazusa ya sode uragaesu doyōboshi*

---

I doubt I will sleep when the moonlight hits the mosquito net

眠らじな蚊帳に月のさす時は
*nemuraji na kachō ni tsuki no sasu toki wa*

# SUMMER

water babbling
  oh! the coolness of the sounds from a tiny flume

涼々と筧の音のすゞしさよ
*sōsō to kakehi no oto no suzushisa yo*

red and white lotus
  blooming in a mortar

紅白の蓮擂鉢に開きけり
*kōhaku no hasu suribachi ni hirakikeri*

lonely though I be
  the moonflower is at its peak

淋しくもまた夕顔のさかりかな
*samishiku mo mata yūgao no sakari kana*

the evening sun out back
  the dry riverbed heat

夕日さす裏は礫のあつさかな
*yūhi sasu ura wa kawara atsusa kana*

even the noon grass lies still
    blazing sun

午時の草もゆるがず照る日かな
*hirudoki no kusa mo yurugazu teru hi kana*

summer weight loss
    burned by the sun
        will the itinerant monk achieve *satori*

夏痩せて日に焦けて雲水の果はいかに
*natsu yasete hi ni yakete unsui no hate wa ikani*

crepe myrtle
    known in the floating world as a sign of passion

百日紅浮世は熱きものと知りぬ
*sarusuberi ukiyo wa atsuki mono to shirinu*

solitude;
    I hole up in summer
        letting my beard grow out

獨身や髭を生して夏に籠る
*hitorimi ya hige o hayashite natsu ni komoru*

high tide;
    as I cool myself
        the moon rises

滿潮や涼んで居れば月が出る
*manchō ya suzundeoreba tsuki ga deru*

---

**First Love**

from this year forward
    shall I copy summer sutras?
        thus I wonder

今年より夏書せんとぞ思ひ立つ
*kotoshi yori gegaki sen to zo omoitatsu*

## First Love

alone
  hiding her face behind a fan
    uncertain

獨り顔を團扇でかくす不審なり
*hitori kao o uchiwa de kakusu fushin nari*

## Love's Parting

the morning after;
  the bamboo-grass field out back is thick with dew

きぬぎぬや裏の篠原露多し
*kinuginu ya ura no shinohara tsuya ōshi*

## Interrupted Love

the bridge collapses
  deep in love during the ceaseless rains of May

橋落ちて戀中絶えぬ五月雨
*hashi ochite koi naka taenu satsukiame*

SUMMER

## Frustrated Love

early summer rain;
the mirror clouds over
what bitterness

五月雨や鏡曇りて恨めしき
*samidare ya kagami kumorite urameshiki*

## Dead Love

rebirth is also melancholy
"amnesia grass"

生れ代るも物憂からましわすれ草
*umarekawaru mo monoukaremashi wasuregusa*

a forlorn bower
thistles, tiger lilies, and the like bloom

亭寂寞薊鬼百合なんど咲く
*chin sekibaku azami oniyuri nando saku*

## Swords

a masterless samurai
his sword rusty
little cuckoo

浪人の刀錆びたり時鳥
*rōnin no katana sabitari hototogisu*

## Swimming

tanned faces
red headbands
people swimming

顔黒く鉢巻赤し泳ぐ人
*kao kuroku hachimaki akashi oyogu hito*

## Swimming

a naked teacher
sitting cross-legged
the swimming hole

裸體なる先生胡坐す水泳所
*ratai naru sensei kozasu suieisho*

## Swimming

emerging after a swim
surprising a water sprite
summer heat

泳ぎ上がり河童驚く暑かな
*oyogiagari kappa odoroku atsusa kana*

---

## Swimming

in a turbid river
the children gather
swimming

泥川に小兒つどいて泳ぎけり
*dorogawa ni shōni tsudoite oyogikeri*

---

## Characters

writing sutras in summer
an Ōbaku monk
named Sokuhi

夏書する黃檗の僧名は卽非
*gegakisuru ōbaku no sō na wa Sokuhi*[3]

## Chanting

from next door come the sounds of chanting
    summer moon

隣より謠ふて來たり夏の月
*tonari yori utōte kitari natsu no tsuki*

through green leaves in profusion
    the banner of a hamlet in sight

靑葉勝に見ゆる小村の幟かな
*aobagachi ni miyuru komura no nobori kana*

the high priest gains weight effortlessly;
    seasonal clothing change

埒もなく禪師肥たり更衣
*rachi mo naku zenji koetari koromogae*

under a carpet of young leaves;
    the sound of water

埋もれて若葉の中や水の音
*uzumorete wakaba no naka ya mizu no oto*

*108*

myriad shadows under the Chinese parasol trees
    a folding stool

影多き梧桐に据る床几かな
*kage ōki gotō ni sueru shōgi kana*

your younger sister's thin hand struggles
    a sushi stone

扛げ兼て妹が手細し鮓の石
*agekanete imo ga te hososhi sushi no ishi*

a doctor of Chinese medicine;
    orange blossoms at the gate

漢方や柑子花さく門構
*kanpō ya kōji hana saku mongamae*

leaning on a wall
    fireflies crawling its length—
        a broom

立て懸て螢這ひけり草箒
*tatekakete hotaru haikeri kusabōki*

a snail waving its eye stalks at the edge of the well

でゞ蟲の角ふり立てゝ井戸の端
*dedemushi no tsuno furitatete ido no hata*

---

in a reservoir
    frogs vie with lusty croaking
        April

溜池に蛙鬭ふ卯月かな
*tameike ni kaeru tatakau uzuki kana*

---

bamboo shoots;
    unexpected through a hedge

筍や思ひがけなき垣根より
*takenoko ya omoigakenaki kakine yori*

new-growth bamboo;
   beside an anonymous gravestone

若竹や名も知らぬ人の墓の傍
*wakatake ya na mo shiranu hito no haka no soba*

---

cracking a whip
   dust rises from a horse cart;
      early summer

鞭鳴す馬車の埃や麥の秋
*muchi narasu basha no hokori ya mugi no aki*

---

though I thought to cross
   no bridge spans the valley
      a cuckoo

渡らんとして谷に橋なし閑古鳥
*wataran toshite tani ni hashi nashi kankodori*

---

writing "soaking in a bath strewn with orchid blossoms"
   I'm a poet

蘭湯に浴すと書て詩人なり
*rantō ni yokusu to kaite shijin nari*[4]

a rancid, damp wooden sushi cooling bowl
   snails

鮓桶の乾かで臭し蝸牛
*sushioke no kawakade kusashi katatsumuri*

eating sweet rice wrapped in bamboo leaves on a night train;
      a tradesman from Zeze

粽食ふ夜汽車や膳所の小商人
*chimaki kuu yogisha ya Zeze no koakindo*

early summer rain;
   unfolding a narrow-sleeved kimono
      a *sake* stain

五月雨や小袖をほどく酒のしみ
*samidare ya kosode o hodoku sake no shimi*

flies from horses, flies from cattle
   ugh! this inn

馬の蠅牛の蠅來る宿屋かな
*uma no hae ushi no hae kuru yadoya kana*

## SUMMER

open for mosquitoes
nothing but mouth
a toad's face

蚊にあけて口許りなり蟇の面
*ka ni akete kuchi bakari nari gama no tsura*

silently, the mosquito stabs deep;
Tabaruzaka

鳴きもせでぐさと刺す蚊や田原坂
*naki mo sede gusa to sasu ka ya Tabaruzaka*[5]

near a thicket
bamboo shoots protrude from under the verandah

藪近し椽の下より筍が
*yabu chikashi en no shita yori takenoko ga*

difficulty sleeping
all night long at the gate
a water rail

寐苦しき門を夜すがら水鶏かな
*negurushiki mon o yosu gara kuina kana*

*113*

threshing colza seed face to face;
    a couple together

菜種打つ向ひ合せや夫婦同志
*natane utsu mukaiawase ya fūfu dōshi*

---

after wheat reaping
    ever come the swallows for the gleanings

麥を刈るあとを頻りに燕かな
*mugi o karu ato o shikiri ni tsubame kana*

---

Wen Yuke;
    eating bamboo shoots and painting bamboo

文與可や笋を食ひ竹を畫く
*Bun Yoka ya takenoko o kui take o kaku*[6]

---

pouring down as if to storm the castle with flood;
    May rains

水攻の城落ちんとす五月雨
*mizuzeme no shiro ochin to su satsukiame*

through the main castle gate come the Minamoto
 wind in early summer verdure

大手より源氏寄せたり青嵐
*ōte yori Genji yosetari aoarashi*

***

a young lass
 her illness somewhat lessened
  given water

撫子に病閑あつて水くれぬ
*nadeshiko ni byō kan atte mizu kurenu*

***

sudden summer shower;
 myriad houses in the teeming market

夕立や犇めく市の十万家
*yūdachi ya hishimeku ichi no jūman ya*

## Staying in Kamakura in early autumn

lantern;
    on a short night
        few shadows are thrown

行燈や短かゝりし夜の影ならず
*andon ya mijikakarishi yo no kage narazu*

---

the young leaves are out
    I am apt to be holed up in my study

若葉して籠り勝なる書齋かな
*wakaba shite komorigachi naru shosai kana*

---

## Kumamoto Higher School autumn *zatsuei*[7] Chemistry Lab

chemistry
    magical arts begetting fireworks

化學とは花火を造る術ならん
*kagaku to wa hanabi o tsukuru jutsu naran*

cloud spires spanning a windless sea

雲の峰風なき海を渡りけり
*kumo no mine kaze naki umi o watarikeri*

---

red sun
    the heat as it sinks into the sea

赤き日の海に落込む暑かな
*akaki hi no umi ni ochikomu atsusa kana*

---

I dwell in the capital
    its skies oppressive;
        October

空狭き都に住むや神無月
*sora semaki miyako ni sumu ya kannazuki*[8]

---

slamming open the sliding window
    the short summer-night sky yields to dawn

引窓をからりと空の明け易き
*hikimado o karari to sora no akeyasuki*

foolish you may be
    yet you, alone, are cool

愚かければ獨りすゞしくおはします
*orokakereba hitori suzushiku owashimasu*

---

listening alone;
    the wild cries of an old nightingale in summer

ひとりきくや夏鶯の亂鳴
*hitori kiku ya natsu uguisu no midarenaki*

---

bat-like umbrella;
    an itinerant geisha in a one-horse town

蝙蝠や一筋町の旅藝者
*kōmori ya hitosuji machi no tabigeisha*

SUMMER

in a glass bowl
   strawberries shed the dew

玻璃盤に露のしたゝる苺かな
*hariban ni tsuyu no shitaruru ichigo kana*

pale mosquito netting
   blown hard into my cool face

蚊帳青く涼しき顔にふきつける
*kaya aoku suzushiki kao ni fukitsukeru*

rose petals scatter;
   I weary of reading Tennyson's poetry

薔薇ちるや天似孫の詩見厭たり
*bara chiru ya Tenison no uta miakitari*

napping and snoozing
   I am Monogusa Tarō

楽寝畫寝われは物草太郎なり
*rakune hirune ware wa Monogusa Tarō nari*[9]

cloud peaks corralling the lightning tower overhead

雲の峰雷を封じて聳えけり
*kumo no mine rai o fūjite sobiekeri*

on this day, a boat enters the canal;
    cloud peaks

船此日運河に入るや雲の峰
*fune kono hi unga ni iru ya kumo no mine*

down to a lotus leaf drops a spider—
    I burn some incense

蓮の葉に蜘蛛下りけり香を焚く
*hasu no ha ni kumo kudarikeri kō o taku*

pearls in her hair and scantily clad
    such coolness

髪に眞珠肌あらはなる涼しさよ
*kami ni shinju hada arawa naru suzushisa yo*

## SUMMER

little cuckoo
   yet, I'm stuck in the privy
      unable to leave

時鳥厠半ばに出かねたり
*hototogisu kawaya nakaba ni dekanetari*

---

silently reading sutras
   while below
      lotus pond susurrations

看經の下は蓮池の戰かな
*kankin no shita wa renchi no soyogi kana*

---

among the white lotus sleeps the Buddha
   down falls a chevron singing stone

白蓮に仏眠れり磬落ちて
*byakuren ni hotoke nemureri kei ochite*

---

a small patch blooming in a field
   lotus blossoms fill the window

田の中に一坪咲いて窓の蓮
*ta no naka ni hitotsubo saite mado no hasu*

daybreak;
    the sun two or three feet o'er the lotus

明くる夜や蓮を放れて二三尺
*akuru yo ya hasu o hanarete ni san jaku*

---

holes in a stone bridge;
    lotus blossoms on the other side

石橋の穴や蓮ある向側
*ishibashi no ana ya hasu aru mukōgawa*

---

droplets fly scattering o'er the ferns
    fresh water

したゝりは歯朶に飛び散る清水かな
*shitatari wa shida ni tobichiru shimizu kana*

---

water trickles through the cwm mosses
    cooling the heart of the world

苔清水天下の胸を冷やしけり
*kokeshimizu tenka no mune o hiyashikeri*

SUMMER

the illusion of moving stones on the bottom
clear water

底の石動いて見ゆる清水哉
*soko no ishi ugoite miyuru shimizu kana*

standing at a precipice
fresh water dripping down the clefts

懸崖に立つ間したゝる清水哉
*kengai ni tatsu ma shitataru shimizu kana*

a wicker valise;
water trickles through the cwm mosses toward
the barrier

兩掛や關のこなたの苔清水
*ryōgake ya seki no konata no kokeshimizu*

a fragrant camphor tree;
water trickles through the cwm mosses outside town

樟の香や村のはづれの苔清水
*kusu no ka ya mura no hazure no koke shimizu*

*123*

through the clear water;
   small footprints

澄みかゝる清水や小き足の跡
*sumikakaru shimizu ya chisaki ashi no ato*

shining in the early autumn breeze
   a spider's thread

立つ秋の風にひかるよ蜘蛛の糸
*tatsu aki no kaze ni hikaru yo kumo no ito*

mid-day colors overflow the cryptomeria hedge
   crepe myrtle

杉垣に晝をこぼれて百日紅
*sugigaki ni hiru o koborete sarusuberi*

a short night
   without even exchanging words

短夜を交す言葉もなかりけり
*mijikayo o kawasu kotoba mo nakarikeri*

even the couple's mosquito net will soon seem too intimate

二人寐の蚊帳も程なく狭からん
*futarine no kaya mo hodo naku semakaran*

early summer rain;
  people coming, long-legged in their *hakama*

五月雨やももだち高く來る人
*samidare ya momodachi takaku kitaru hito*

the roofless gate of the abattoir;
  a summer grove

屠牛場の屋根なき門や夏木立
*togyūba no yane naki mon ya natsu kodachi*

## Walls

my back against the wall
  might that cool my naked body?

壁に脊を涼しからんの裸哉
*kabe ni se o suzushikaran no hadaka kana*[10]

## In Kamibayashi

through the mosquito net
    I see the green mountains and stands of cedar

蚊帳越しに見る山青し杉木立
*kayagoshi ni miru yama aoshi sugi kodachi*

snails;
    all May spent on a butterbur stalk

蝸牛や五月をわたるふきの茎
*dedemushi ya gogatsu o wataru fuki no kuki*

# Autumn

## 秋

poetry written on lanterns—
   an autumn journey

行燈にいろはかきけり秋の旅
*andon ni iroha kakikeri aki no tabi*

autumn fades
   a lone persimmon lies where it fell
      in the frost

秋さびて霜に落けり柿一つ
*aki sabite shimo ni ochikeri kaki hitotsu*

persimmon leaves;
   each one dappled by the moonlight

柿の葉や一つ一つに月の影
*kaki no ha ya hitotsu hitotsu ni tsuki no kage*

accompanying autumn's breezes
my first white hair

秋風と共に生へしか初白髪
*akikaze to tomo ni haeshika hatsushiraga*[1]

**Lamentations for a Wife**

morning glory
yours was a life that had but only just blossomed

朝貌や咲た許りの命哉
*asagao ya saita bakari no inochi kana*[2]

**Lamentations for a Wife**

after today
to whom shall I compare it?
the autumn moon

今日よりは誰に見立ん秋の月
*kyō yori wa dare ni mitaten aki no tsuki*

# AUTUMN

accustomed to the bowstring's twang
    little birds come a-twittering

弦音になれて來て鳴く小鳥かな
*tsuruoto ni narete kite naku kotori kana*

---

autumn cicadas
    their thrumming imbued with a reluctance to die

秋の蟬死度くもなき聲音かな
*aki no semi shinitaku mo naki kowane kana*

---

an old man and woman
    a melancholy autumn equinox

爺と婆淋しき秋の彼岸かな
*Jiji to baba sabishiki aki no higan kana*

lightning;
  now and again is the cataract visible

稲妻や折々見ゆる瀧の底
*inazuma ya oriori miyuru taki no soko*

a bagworm's cry;
  how hard the wait for the long night to break

簑虫のなくや長夜の明けかねて
*minomushi no naku ya nagayo no akekanete*[3]

aboard a boat;
  geese winging through the night sky
    who will arrive first?

便船や夜を行く雁のあとや先
*binsen ya yo o iku kari no ato ya saki*

AUTUMN

the orchids' fragrance;
    I step out the gate to the flag of the rising sun

蘭の香や門を出づれば日の御旗
*ran no ka ya mon o izureba hi no mihata*

in the morning cold
    a man peddling some star anise

朝寒に樒賣り來る男かな
*asasamu ni shikimi urikuru otoko kana*

looking up
the autumnal sky
like a towering castle

見上ぐれば城屹として秋の空
*miagureba shirokitsu toshite aki no sora*

about the cliff base bloom Tatarian aster—
between the rocks

崖下に紫苑咲きけり石の間
*gakeshita ni shion sakikeri ishi no ai*

alone and uncertain
what's the acolyte's fortune?
autumn's gloaming

獨りわびて僧何占ふ秋の暮
*hitori wabite sō nani uranau aki no kure*

an old horse's bony ass is quite embarrassing
all those autumn flies

痩馬の尻こそはゆし秋の蠅
*yaseuma no shiri koso hayushi aki no hae*

# AUTUMN

a mountain in fall
　　two temples nestled on its southern exposure

秋の山南を向いて寺二つ
*aki no yama minami o muite tera futatsu*

the train has passed
　　lapping waves of undulating rice in paddies

汽車去つて稲の波うつ畑かな
*kisha satte ina no nami utsu hatake kana*

autumn sky
　　nameless mountains climb ever higher

秋の空名もなき山の愈高し
*aki no sora na mo naki yama no iyoyo takashi*

right, left, and forward
　　verdant bamboo
　　　　clear autumn water

三方は竹緑なり秋の水
*sanbō wa take midori nari aki no mizu*

# SŌSEKI NATSUME'S COLLECTED HAIKU

a massive thicket;
   in numbers uncountable
      dragonflies take wing

大藪や數を盡して蜻蛉とぶ
*ōyabu ya kazu o tsukushite tonbo tobu*

---

swallows heading south perchance to return home
   wild, grassy plain

歸燕いづくにか歸る草茫々
*kien izu kuni ka kaeru kusa bōbō*

---

standing naked in a withering wind
   temple guardians

凩に裸で御はす仁王哉
*kogarashi ni hadaka de owasu niō kana*

---

copious drink
   plucking white chrysanthemums
      perchance we might dance

飲む事一斗白菊折つて舞はん哉
*nomu koto itto shiragiku otte mawan kana*

*134*

yellow and white chrysanthemum petals
the night sky in my wine
I want for nothing

黄菊白菊酒中の天地貧ならず
*kigiku shiragiku shuchū no tenchi hin narazu*

chrysanthemum fragrance;
those Jin Dynasty hermits truly loved their wine

菊の香や晋の高士は酒が好き
*kiku no ka ya Shin no kōshi wa sake ga suki*[4]

maple leaves scatter in a green-drenched bamboo grove
five or six

紅葉ちる竹緑ぬれて五六枚
*momiji chiru chikuen nurete go-rokumai*

to even the mountain's foot has autumn made its way—
a waterfall's sound

麓にも秋立ちにけり瀧の音
*fumoto ni mo aki tachinikeri taki no oto*

chilly;
    lambent lamplight
      a waterfall's sound

うそ寒や灯火ゆるぐ瀧の音
*usosamu ya tomoshibi yurugu taki no oto*

clouds here and there obscure the crags above
    brilliant autumn foliage

雲處々岩に喰ひ込む紅葉哉
*kumo achikochi iwa ni kuikomu momiji kana*

common ditch reeds
    just where the river bends

蘆の花夫より川は曲がりけり
*ashi no hana sore yori kawa wa magarikeri*

the westering sun;
    comes the sigh of a distant autumn wind

日の入や秋風遠く鳴つて來る
*hi no iri ya akikaze tōku natte kuru*

## AUTUMN

dragonfly;
    a mere two inches from the piling

蜻蛉や杭を離るゝ事二寸
*seirei ya kui o hanaruru koto ni sun*

giant katydid startled;
    the ceaseless sound of a flute

轡虫すはやと絶ぬ笛の音
*kutsuwamushi suwaya to taenu fue no oto*

a deep ravine;
    when I go out
        the autumn sky is so small

谷深し出る時秋の空小し
*tani fukashi deru toki aki no sora chisashi*

in the morning cold passing under the torii
    a lone figure

朝寒の鳥居をくゞる一人哉
*asasamu no torii o kuguru hitori kana*

whose house might this be?
nothing but white chrysanthemums in disarray

誰が家ぞ白菊ばかり亂るゝは
*ta ga ie zo shiragiku bakari midaruru wa*

threshing the rice under a sour persimmon tree
husband and wife

澁柿の下に稲こく夫婦かな
*shibugaki no shita ni ine koku fūfu kana*

gathering mushrooms;
the red of the torii in Komatsuyama

茸狩や鳥居の赤き小松山
*takegari ya torii no akaki Komatsuyama*

silver pampas grass
take a leak and lose your horse

花芒小便すれば馬逸す
*hanasusuki shōben sureba uma issu*

the autumn mountains
   quietly the clouds pass by

秋の山静かに雲の通りけり
*aki no yama shizuka ni kumo no tōrikeri*

---

on either side of a valley river
   narrow rice fields
      shorn

谷川の左右に細き刈田哉
*tanigawa no sayū ni hosoki karita kana*

---

a woman washing potatoes
   an alabaster mountain cottage

芋洗ふ女の白き山家かな
*imo arau onna no shiroki yamaga kana*

cackling of hens;
　　myriad scattered hamlets in the autumn rain

鶏鳴くや小村々々の秋の雨
*tori naku ya komura komura no aki no ame*

---

in the autumn rain;
　　a mountain cottage, its lanterns dark

秋雨に行燈暗き山家かな
*akisame ni andon kuraki yamaga kana*

---

seeking lodging all alone in a widow's hut
　　frigid autumn night

孀の家獨り宿かる夜寒かな
*yamome no ya hitori yado karu yosamu kana*

---

put the visitor in the drawing room to sleep
　　frigid autumn night

客人を書院に寐かす夜寒哉
*kyakujin o shoin ni nekasu yosamu kana*

# AUTUMN

autumn rain
abed in some inn
thinking about tomorrow

秋雨に明日思はるゝ旅寐哉
*akisame ni asu omowaruru tabine kana*

has autumn come to the world?
this straw raincape and bamboo hat

世は秋となりしにやこの簑と笠
*yo wa aki to narishini ya kono mino to kasa*

the mountains resound;
forceful, rushing cataract
on the autumn wind

山鳴るや瀑とうとうと秋の風
*yama naru ya taki tōtō to aki no kaze*

myriad mountains shed a drenching rainfall;
autumn cataracts

満山の雨を落すや秋の瀧
*manzan no ame o otosu ya aki no taki*

*141*

an immense boulder;
  riven asunder
    autumn cataract

大岩や二つとなつて秋の瀧
*ōiwa ya futatsu to natte aki no taki*

---

white cataract;
  between the black boulders
    vines in autumn colors

白瀧や黑き岩間の蔦紅葉
*shirataki ya kuroki iwama no tsutamomiji*

---

above the dark waterfall, the sun shines bright
  dappled fall colors

瀑暗し上を日の照るむら紅葉
*taki kurashi ue o hi no teru muramomiji*

---

the clouds come and they go
  autumn foliage at the waterfall

雲來り雲去る瀑の紅葉かな
*kumo kitari kumo saru taki no momiji kana*

the mist clears
    the waterfall comes gradually into view

霧晴るゝ瀑は次第に現はるゝ
*kiri haruru taki wa shidai ni arawaruru*

drying maize;
    a solitary house in the valley

唐黍を干すや谷間の一軒家
*tōkibi o hosu ya tanima no ikkenya*

the harvest moon;
    distant lies my family home
        beyond my shadow

名月や故郷遠き影法師
*meigetsu ya furusato tōki kagebōshi*

a late autumn gale shatters the waterfall
    here at my very feet

野分吹く瀑砕け散る脚下より
*nowaki fuku taki kudakechiru kyakka yori*

cataracts far and near
in valleys and on mountain peaks
late autumn gale

瀧遠近谷も尾上も野分哉
*taki ochikochi tani mo onoe mo nowaki kana*

here and there a tree
already in fall colors;
this shrine gateway

一木二木はや紅葉るやこの鳥居
*ichimoku nimoku haya momizuru ya kono torii*

**Ill when travelling**

as autumn departs;
clouds on the verge of vanishing
linger

行秋や消えなんとして殘る雲
*yuku aki ya kienan toshite nokoru kumo*

AUTUMN

uneven shadows of three pine trees
    a moonlit night

影参差松三本の月夜哉
*kage shinshi matsu sanbon no tsukiyo kana*

late autumn storm
    the morning birds have already taken wing

野分して朝鳥早く立ちけらし
*nowaki shite asadori hayaku tachikerashi*

October with its intermittent rains
    no letters come from you

十月のしぐれて文も参らせず
*jūgatsu no shigurete fumi mo mairasezu*

the October moon;
    evermore fantastic it grows

十月の月ややうやう凄くなる
*jūgatsu no tsuki ya yōyō sugokunaru*

### Hakata Park

a thousand pine trees in early autumn
   swaying

初秋の千本の松動きけり
*hatsuaki no senbon no matsu ugokikeri*

### Tenpaizan Mountain

looking upward
   on the summit
      autumn pines stand tall

見上げたる尾の上に秋の松高し
*miagetaru o no ue ni aki no matsu takashi*

AUTUMN

## Dazaifu Tenjin Shrine

from the arched bridge they look so small
　　lotuses

反橋の小さく見ゆる芙蓉哉
*soribashi no chiisaku miyuru fuyō kana*

---

## Bairinji Temple

preaching the gist of the *Blue Cliff Record*
　　long night in a mountain temple

碧巖を提唱す山内の夜ぞ長き
*Hekigan o teishōsu sannai no yo zo nagaki*[5]

---

a traveller seen in the lightning
　　the great plain

稲妻に行手の見えぬ廣野かな
*inazuma ni yukute no mienu hirono kana*

autumnal breeze;
    temples in the capital toll their bells

秋風や京の寺々鐘を撞く
*akikaze ya kyō no teradera kane o tsuku*

---

the shadow of a pillar in the corridor;
    moon on the sea

廻廊の柱の影や海の月
*kairō no hashira no kage ya umi no tsuki*

---

neither wine nor poetry
    the tranquility of the moon

酒なくて詩なくて月の静かさよ
*sake nakute shi nakute tsuki no shizukasa yo*

---

pounding cloth to a sheen
    perchance a gift to her husband
        a small package

衣擣つて郎に贈らん小包で
*kinu utte rō ni okuran kozutsumi de*

AUTUMN

alabaster wall;
 facing north
  autumn's first falling paulownia leaf

白壁や北に向ひて桐一葉
*shirakabe ya kita ni mukaite kirihitoha*

the scattering willow leaves
 Chang'an is the autumn capitol

柳ちりて長安は秋の都かな
*yanagi chirite Chōan wa aki no miyako kana*[6]

a solitary horseman making his escape
 bush clover field

落ち延びて只一騎なり萩の原
*ochinobite tada ikki nari hagi no hara*

fragrant orchids;
 shall I learn calligraphy from Wang's sacred writings?

蘭の香や聖教帖を習はんか
*ran no ka ya shōgyōjō o narawan ka*[7]

*149*

behind me they cry
before me they cry;
quails

後に鳴き又先に鳴き鶉かな
*ato ni naki mata saki ni naki uzura kana*

with gay abandon the ivy crawls upward
outhouse

無雑作に蔦這上る厠かな
*muzōsa no tsuta hainoboru kawaya kana*

a wandering performer;
Koharu and Jihei at autumn's gloaming

祭文や小春治兵衛に暮るゝ秋
*saimon ya Koharu Jihei ni kururu aki*[8]

a meditation hall where I wasted away as autumn's night fell

僧堂で痩せたる我に秋暮れぬ
*sōdō de yasetaru ware ni aki kurenu*

working her loom
    a widow at twenty
        autumn departs

機を織る孀二十で行く秋や
*hata o oru yamome hatachi de yuku aki ya*

sunset;
    lingering on the five-story pagoda in autumn

日の入や五重の塔に残る秋
*hinoiri ya gojū no tō ni nokoru aki*

departing autumn;
    slanting sunlight on the verandah

行く秋や椽にさし込む日は斜
*yuku aki ya en ni sashikomu hi wa naname*

the broad plain
    beyond my gate
        a moonless night bright with stars

原廣し吾門前の星月夜
*hara hiroshi ware monzen no hoshizukiyo*

## Remembering Kohaku

Kohaku should be synonymous with autumn

古白とは秋につけたる名なるべし
*Kohaku to wa aki ni tsuketaru na narubeshi*[9]

## Love's Parting

the morning after;
the bamboo-grass field out back is thick with dew

きぬぎぬや裏の篠原露多し
*kinuginu ya ura no shinohara tsuya ōshi*

## Stealthy Love

secret petitions on colorful strands tangled together

人に言へぬ願の糸の亂れかな
*hito ni ienu negai no ito no midare kana*

AUTUMN

## Stealthy Love

your name;
I write it on an inkstone
and wash it away

君が名や硯に書いては洗ひ消す
*kimi ga na ya suzuri ni kaite wa araikesu*

shadowy fish strike into algaed depths
water in autumn

藻ある底に魚の影さす秋の水
*mo aru soko ni uo no kage sasu aki no mizu*

autumn mountains
pine trees in sharp relief
the westering sun

秋の山松明かに入日かな
*aki no yama matsu akaraka ni irihi kana*

"autumn is passing"
a mountain youth pushes open a window

秋行くと山僮窓を排しいふ
*akiyuku to sandō mado o haishi iu*

---

an autumn fly
captured and then released

秋の蠅握つて而して放したり
*aki no hae nigitte soshite hanshitari*

---

inauspicious;
the bride shattered the vase at autumn's gloaming

生憎や嫁瓶を破る秋の暮
*ainiku ya yome bin o yaburu aki no kure*

---

a horse-washing tub;
steam rising from the water
chilly morning

馬盥や水烟して朝寒し
*badarai ya mizukemurishite asa samushi*

AUTUMN

in the sky
    the remnant of fall clouds goes by
        a lone observer

空に一片秋の雲行く見る一人
*sora ni ippen aki no kumo yuku miru hitori*

---

autumn's soaring sky!
    would that I were riding the white clouds

秋高し吾白雲に乗らんと思ふ
*akitakashi ware shirakumo ni noran to mou*

---

autumn's chill against my skin;
    yet, I must sit formally

肌寒や膝を崩さず坐るべく
*hadazamu ya hiza o kuzusazu suwarubeku*

the sound of overflowing *go* stones scattering on a gelid night

盛り崩す碁石の音の夜寒し
*morikuzusu goishi no oto no yoru samushi*

a hole in the wall
surely I'll catch cold as the temperature drops

壁の穴風を引くべく稍寒し
*kabe no ana kaze o hikubeku yaya samushi*

## Characters

a guest with a poem
ink flows from the ground inkstick
before the moon

客に賦あり墨磨り流す月の前
*kyaku ni fu ari sumi surinagasu tsuki no mae*

## Engaku-ji Temple

the cool bell tolls—
　　Engaku-ji Temple

冷かな鐘をつきけり圓覺寺
*hiyayakana kane o tsukikeri Enkakuji*

## Engaku-ji Temple

in a mountain temple, ruing the post-bath cooling;
　　early autumn morning

山寺に湯ざめを悔る今朝の秋
*yamadera ni yuzame o kuiru kesa no aki*

cacophonous cries
　　the Walker's cicadas die today

鳴き立てゝつくつく法師死ぬる日ぞ
*nakitatete tsukutsukubōshi shinuru hi zo*

as the boat departs
   the sound of imprecations
      heavy fog

船出るとのゝしる聲す深き霧
*fune deru to nonoshiru koe su fukaki kiri*

---

**Arriving in Kumamoto on 10 September**

arriving in southern Kyushu
   the persimmons are already ripe

南九州に入つて柿既に熟す
*minami Kyūshū ni haitte kaki sudeni jukusu*

---

covered with bush clover and tangled in pampas grass
   the old capital

萩に伏し薄にみだれ故里は
*hagi ni fushi susuki ni midare furusato wa*

# AUTUMN

praying mantis
   what has put you in high dudgeon?

蟷螂の何を以てか立腹す
*tōrō no nani o motte ka rippukusu*

---

crickets
   abruptly chirping
      suddenly silent

蟋のふと鳴き出しぬ鳴きやみぬ
*kōrogi no futo nakidashinu nakiyaminu*

---

autumnal breeze;
   the old satchel set high on a shelf

秋風や棚に上げたる古かばん
*akikaze ya tana ni agetaru furu kaban*

---

bright moonlight;
   illiterate, perhaps
      yet still drinking wine

明月や無筆なれども酒は呑む
*meigetsu ya muhitsu naredomo sake wa nomu*

under a bright moon
　　this year we meet again upon a journey

明月に今年も旅で逢ひ申す
*meigetsu ni kotoshi mo tabi de aimōsu*

the dead of night
　　how lonely you must be
　　　　wonderful moon

眞夜中は淋しからうに御月樣
*mayonaka wa samishikarō ni otsukisama*

crickets!
　　it's autumn whether you chirrup or not

蟋よ秋ぢゃ鳴かうが鳴くまいが
*kōrogi yo aki ja nakō ga nakumai ga*

autumn's gloaming
　　travelling alone is truly loathsome

秋の暮一人旅とて嫌はるゝ
*aki no kure hitoritabi tote kirawaruru*

without even a "look here"
    the moon appears

これ見よと云はぬ許りに月が出る
*kore miyo to iwanu bakari ni tsuki ga deru*

a cold bath on a cold autumn morning
    how truly trying

朝寒の冷水浴を難んずる
*asasamu no reisuiyoku o katanzuru*

**Leaving my wife behind and going alone to Higo**

going to a moon viewing
    I have forgotten my wife

月に行く漱石妻を忘れたり
*tsuki ni yuku Sōseki tsuma o wasuretari*

passing a long night with an untroubled companion

長き夜を平氣な人と合宿す
*nagaki yo o heiki na hito to gasshukusu*

there are travellers who eat large meals of somewhat chilly food

うそ寒み大めしを食ふ旅客あり
*usosamumi ōmeshi o kuu ryokaku ari*

---

moonlight pours into the bath area and out they come
    Heike crabs

月さして風呂場へ出たり平家蟹
*tsuki sashite furoba e detari Heikegani*[10]

---

someone set up the scarecrow
    regal sparrows

某は案山子にて候雀どの
*soregashi wa kakashi nite sōrō suzume-dono*

---

yanking the striking-log rope
    mere frustration born of *ennui*

鳴子引くは只退窟で困る故
*naruko hiku wa tada taikutsu de komaru yue*

## AUTUMN

if you don't bite, I promise you won't die
  autumn mosquitoes

刺さずんば已まずと誓ふ秋の蚊や
*sasazunba yamazu to chikau aki no ka ya*


autumn mosquitoes
  don't underestimate them in dream

秋の蚊と夢油断ばしし給ふな
*aki no ka to yume yudan bashi shitamau na*


late autumn storm
  a praying mantis borne upon the wind
    through the window

野分して蟷螂を窓に吹き入るゝ
*nowaki shite tōrō o mado ni fukiiruru*

their northern face
    flashed by lightning;
        black clouds

北側を稲妻燒くや黒き雲
*kitagawa o inazuma yaku ya kuroki kumo*

---

the sound of a spider dropping to the matting
    a thin lamp flame in autumn

蛛落ちて疊に音す秋の灯細し
*kumo ochite tatami ni otosu aki no hi hososhi*

## AUTUMN

once
    drunk on the new year's *sake*
      I was beset with regrets

ある時は新酒に酔て悔多き
*aru toki wa shinshu ni yoite kui ōki*

Chinese parasol open o'er chrysanthemums
    a new residence

傘を菊にさしたり新屋敷
*karakasa o kiku ni sashitari shinyashiki*

autumn's advent without so much as a warning
    under my mosquito net

來る秋のことわりもなく蚊帳の中
*kuru aki no kotowari mo naku kaya no naka*

moonlight seeping through the withered paulownia
    so many shadows

桐かれて洩れ來る月の影多し
*kiri karete morekuru tsuki no kage ōshi*

## Four fellow travelers upon hearing they would be riding in a horse-drawn wagon

crammed into a small horse-drawn wagon—
    full rice heads

小き馬車に積み込まれけり稲の花
*chisaki basha ni tsumikomarekeri ine no hana*

begonias in twilight
    the butterflies are indifferent

夕暮の秋海棠に蝶うとし
*yūgure no shūkaidō ni chō utoshi*

to and fro
    a single butterfly among the chrysanthemums

離れては寄りては菊の蝶一つ
*hanarete wa yorite wa kiku no chō hitotsu*

the barbarians were haughty and quick to startle
  wild geese honking

胡兒驕つて驚きやすし雁の声
*Koji ogotte odoroki yasushi kari no koe*[11]

---

someone striking a fulling block around midnight
  a poem comes unbidden

砧うつ眞夜中頃に句を得たり
*kinuta utsu mayonaka koro ni ku o etari*

---

talking throughout the long night
  two friends

長かれと夜すがら語る二人かな
*nagakare to yo sugara kataru futari kana*

---

a sumo wrestler
  his face etched with worry;
    afternoon rain

相撲取の屈託顔や午の雨
*sumōtori no kuttakugao ya hiru no ame*

during an illness
    heavy rains on the amaranth

病む頃を雁來紅に雨多し
*yamu koro o ganraikō ni ame ōshi*

lodging at a temple for twenty days
    cockscomb still blossoms

寺借りて二十日になりぬ鶏頭花
*tera karite hatsuka ni narinu keitōka*

a hedge trimmed to a uniform height
    cloudless autumn day

生垣の丈かり揃へ晴るゝ秋
*ikegaki no takekari soroe haruru aki*

deep autumn chill
    the wild ocean's hue this time of year

秋寒し此頃あるゝ海の色
*aki samushi kono koro aruru umi no iro*

# AUTUMN

morning glory;
    crawling up toward the towel rack

朝顔や手拭懸に這ひ上る
*asagao ya tenuguikake ni haiagaru*

———

trysting lover's no longer beating a fulling-block tattoo—
    nighttime

逢ふ恋の打たでやみけり小夜砧
*au koi no utade yamikeri sayoginuta*

———

a single cluser of swaying pampas grass;
    in a planter

一株の芒動くや鉢の中
*hitokabu no susuki ugoku ya hachi no naka*

———

a lamp burning in my ailing wife's room
    autumn's gloaming

病妻の閨に灯ともし暮るゝ秋
*byōsai no neya ni hi tomoshi kururu aki*

*169*

a long night;
   a teapot drip-drying in the kitchen

長き夜や土瓶をしたむ臺所
*nagaki yo ya dobin o shitamu daidokoro*

---

chirruping by a decoupage folding screen;
   a cricket

張まぜの屏風になくや蟋蟀
*harimaze no byōbu ni naku ya kirigirisu*

---

owing to illness
   the blossoming lantern flame lengthens the night

病むからに行燈の華の夜を長み
*yamu kara ni andon no ka no yo o nagami*

---

written across the white envelope: "Death Notice"
   it has grown colder

白封に訃音と書いて漸寒し
*hakufū ni fuin to kaite yaya samushi*

# AUTUMN

meeting over this year's *sake*
    a doctor and a seer introduce themselves

落ち合ひて新酒に名乗る醫者易者
*ochiaite shinshu ni nanoru isha ekisha*

I looked at the autumn sun and saw it heartless
    parting

秋の日のつれなく見えし別かな
*aki no hi no tsurenaku mieshi wakare kana*

at a Guan shrine in late autumn
    a smokeless incense bowl

行く秋の關廟の香爐烟なし
*yuku aki no Kan byō no korō kemuri nashi*[12]

using a toothpick on a frosty morning;
    the sink

朝寒の楊子使ふや流し元
*asasamu no yōji tsukau ya nagashimoto*

hastening to the capital in a palanquin
   golden lace

駕舁の京へと急ぐ女郎花
*kagokaki no kyō e to isogu ominaeshi*

---

time and again
   the willows weep their slender leaves
      an ebbing passion

柳散り柳散りつゝ細る戀
*yanagi chiri yanagi chiritsutsu hosoru koi*

---

my illness unrelenting
   squatting down at night in a late autumn storm

病癒えず蹲る夜の野分かな
*yamai iezu uzukumaru yo no nowaki kana*

---

mating dragonflies flitting hither and yon
   over the water

つるんだる蜻蛉飛ぶなり水の上
*tsurundaru tonbo tobu nari mizu no ue*

a hard pear
  paired with a dull paring knife

堅き梨に鈍き刃物を添てけり
*kataki nashi ni nibuki hamono o soetekeri*

---

## Toshita hot springs 4 [of 8] poems

from deep in the valley whence hot springs bubble up
  autumn's first wild storm

温泉湧く谷の底より初嵐
*ideyu waku tani no soko yori hatsuarashi*

---

a mountain village;
  tonight, the eve of autumn
    water's sound

山里や今宵秋立つ水の音
*yamazato ya koyoi akitatsu mizu no oto*

horses out to pasture on a grassy mountain—
    broad autumn sky

草山に馬放ちけり秋の空
*kusayama ni uma hanachikeri aki no sora*

golden lace
    rising up out of the manure

女郎花馬糞について上りけり
*ominaeshi bafun ni tsuite noborikeri*

## Uchinomaki Hot Springs 9 [of 15] poems

no fence prevents it pressing upon the bath tub
    gossamer fog

囲ひあらで湯槽に逼る狭霧かな
*kakoi arade yubune ni semaru sagiri kana*

AUTUMN

from the bath tub
   I look out in all directions;
      rice blossoms

湯槽から四方を見るや稲の花
*yubune kara shihō o miru ya ine no hana*

wishing to depart
   yet seems it won't;
      a wet sparrow

歸らんとして歸らぬ様や濡れ燕
*kaeran toshite kaeranu yō ya nure tsubame*

gazing out the privy window;
   autumn mountains

雪隠の窓から見るや秋の山
*setsuin no mado kara miru ya aki no yama*

the whole day through;
   autumn clouds never leave the mountain's summit

終日や尾の上離れぬ秋の雲
*hinemosu ya o no ue hanarenu aki no kumo*

spilling out of a reaper's basket
wild chrysanthemums

草刈の籃の中より野菊かな
*kusakari no kago no naka yori nogiku kana*

silver dew;
the color of a burnished sickle

白露や研ぎすましたる鎌の色
*shiratsuyu ya togisumashitaru kama no iro*

autumn river
picking up the alabaster stones

秋の川眞白な石を拾ひけり
*aki no kawa mashirona ishi o hiroikeri*

autumn rain
the sound of feeding the fire dry cedar needles

秋雨や杉の枯葉をくべる音
*akisame ya sugi no kareha o kuberu oto*

**Aso Shrine**

a gelid morning
a pilgrimage to an unvarnished shrine

朝寒み白木の宮に詣でけり
*asa samumi shiraki no miya ni mōdekei*

---

**Aso Shrine**

even birds won't fly
warning clapper at the start of the storm season

鳥も飛ばず二百十日の鳴子かな
*tori mo tobazu nihyakutōka no naruko kana*

---

**Losing my way on Mt. Aso and spending the day on fruitless wandering**

standing, damp with volcanic ash;
amidst pampas grass and bush clover

灰に濡れて立つや薄と萩の中
*hai ni nurete tatsu ya susuki to hagi no naka*

a single wild chrysanthemum petal pressed in my notebook

野菊一輪手帳の中に挾みけり
*nogiku ichirin techō no naka ni hasamikeri*

I stand before the washbasin to wash my face;
  shades of autumn

顔洗ふ盥に立つや秋の影
*kao arau tarai ni tatsu ya aki no kage*

the bucket rope broke
  I peer into the well;
    early autumn morning

釣瓶きれて井戸を覗くや今朝の秋
*tsurube kirete ido o nozoku ya kesa no aki*

the hanging scroll shifts restlessly on the rough-painted wall
  autumn wind

荒壁に軸落ちつかず秋の風
*arakabe ni jiku ochitsukazu aki no kaze*

**Farewell**

when the time is ripe even the swallows eventually return

時くれば燕もやがて帰るなり
*toki kureba tsubame mo yagate kaeru nari*

---

**Kumamoto Higher School autumn *zatsuei*[13]**

**School**

entering the stately gate
    buckwheat blossoms

いかめしき門を這入れば蕎麦の花
*ikameshiki mon o haireba soba no hana*

---

**Playing Fields**

emerging from the pines to a sparkling wonder
    dew-bejeweled field

松を出てまばゆくぞある露の原
*matsu o dete mabayuku zo aru tsuyu no hara*

## Library

the book ties have rotted
    rebinding them in the night-chilled storehouse

韋編斷えて夜寒の倉に束ねたる
*ihen taete yosamu no kura ni tabanetaru*

## Honakan Building

hanging hoary oil painting
    autumn butterfly

古ぼけし油繪をかけ秋の蝶
*furubokeshi aburae o kake aki no chō*

## Ethics Lecture

I'm not up to these red things
    chili peppers

赤き物少しは参れ蕃椒
*akaki mono sukoshi wa maire tōgarashi*[14]

**Classroom**

neatly ordered faces, blue with the morning cold—
   desks

朝寒の顔を揃へし机かな
*asasamu no kao o soroeshi tsukue kana*

---

**Classroom**

ruffling the teacher's sparse whiskers;
   autumn breeze

先生の疎髯を吹くや秋の風
*sensei no sozen o fuku ya aki no kaze*

---

**Arboretum**

ignorant of its true name
   the flowers of some plant

本名は頓とわからず草の花
*honmyō wa ton to wakarazu kusa no hana*

### Arboretum

green moss
    why, not even a hint of brown in the stem tips

苔青く末枯るゝべきものもなし
*koke aoku ura karurubeki mono mo nashi*

### Natural Philosophy Lab

the southern window prints a photograph;
    red dragonfly

南窓に寫眞を燒くや赤蜻蛉
*nansō ni shashin o yaku ya akatonbo*

### Chemistry Lab

sponge cucumber fluid in a glass flask;
    about 3,600ml

玻璃瓶に糸瓜の水や二升程
*haribin ni hechima no mizu ya nishō hodo*

AUTUMN

## Zoology Lab

the stuffed and mounted shrike no longer calls
    midday loneliness

剥製の鵙鳴かなくに晝淋し
*hakusei no mozu nakanaku ni hiru samishi*

## Dining Hall

Fan Kuai!
    open the door to rice flavored with mushrooms

樊噲や闥を排して茸の飯
*Han Kai ya tatsu o haishite take no meshi*[15]

## Dining Hall

gluttony at the seat of honor
    yellow chestnut rice

大食を上座に栗の飯黄なり
*ōgui o kamiza ni kuri no meshi ki ari*

### Oratorical Meeting

considered especially flavorful
   persimmons and chestnuts

就中うましと思ふ柿と栗
*nakanzuku umashi to omou kaki to kuri*

### Kendō Meeting

lightning too fast for the eye to catch
   a match decided

稲妻の目にも留らぬ勝負哉
*inazuma no me ni mo tomaranu shōbu kana*

### Judō Match

flutter though it may
   the pampas grass cannot be flattened

靡けども芒を倒し能はざる
*nabikedomo susuki o taoshi atawazaru*

AUTUMN

pitter-patter on a rubber raincoat
    autumn rain

さらさらと護謨の合羽に秋の雨
*sarasara to gomu no kappa ni aki no ame*

looking through the hanging bell pavilion;
    autumn sea

釣鐘をすかして見るや秋の海
*tsurigane o sukashite miru ya aki no umi*

a cat in the chrysanthemums
    oh, get Shen Quan!

菊に猫沈南蘋を招きけり
*kiku ni neko Shen Nanbin o manekikeri*[16]

the shrine wall;
    holding aloft fall colors
        a shrine maiden's sleeves

神垣や紅葉を翳す巫女の袖
*kamigaki ya momiji o kazasu miko no sode*

*185*

SŌSEKI NATSUME'S COLLECTED HAIKU

a duel;
    outside town on a moonless night bright with stars

決闘や町をはなれて星月夜
*kettō ya machi o hanarete hoshizukiyo*

---

a lone person blown by an autumn wind;
    upon the ocean

秋風の一人をふくや海の上
*akikaze no hitori o fuku ya umi no ue*

---

"where is the Picture Gallery?"
    I asked of a person roasting chestnuts

繪所を栗燒く人に尋ねけり
*edokoro o kuri yaku hito ni tazunekeri*

---

hot, wind-blown sand about the foundation
    late autumn gale

礎に砂吹きあつる野分かな
*ishizue ni suna fukiatsuru nowake kana*

AUTUMN

blowing off a creased cloth cap as they pass
late autumn gale

角巾を吹き落し行く野分かな
*kakkin o fukiotoshiyuku nowake kana*

**The Emperor's birthday**

Heavan and earth
there is nowhere not redolent with chrysanthemums

後天後土菊匂はざる處なし
*kōten kōdo kiku niowazaru tokoro nashi*

an Italian roasting chestnuts;
by the roadside

栗を燒く伊太利人や道の傍
*kuri o yaku itarījin ya michi no hata*

Western garb;
ill befitting an autumn casket

筒袖や秋の柩にしたがはず
*tsutsusode ya aki no hitsugi ni shitagawazu*[17]

*187*

not even supplicatory incense to send you off
    autumn's gloaming

手向くべき線香もなくて暮の秋
*tamukubeki senkō mo nakute kure no aki*

---

moving through a city sallowed in fog;
    human shades

霧黄なる市に動くや影法師
*kiri ki naru ichi ni ugoku ya kagebōshi*

---

recalling crickets long ago
    I should return

きりぎりすの昔を忍び帰るべし
*kirigirisu no mukashi o shinobi kaerubeshi*

---

an incessant autumn wind blows;
    old hackberry tree

秋風のしきりに吹くや古榎
*akikaze no shikiri ni fuku ya furuenoki*

## AUTUMN

harvest moon;
    Tōdaiji Temple in the cedars as night deepens

名月や杉に更けたる東大寺
*meigetsu ya sugi ni fuketaru Tōdaiji*

in the shadow of the morning glories' leaves
    cat's eyes

朝皃の葉影に猫の眼玉かな
*asagao no hakage ni neko no medama kana*

breaking off a single white chrysanthemum
    my lonely hermitage

白菊の一本折れて庵淋し
*shiragiku no ippon orete an samishi*

a hanging bell moans incessantly
    late autumn storm

釣鐘のうなる許りに野分かな
*tsurigane no unaru bakari ni nowaki kana*

Amanohashidate;
  a string of pines against the autumn sky

橋立や松一筋に秋の空
*Hashidate ya matsu hitosuji ni aki no sora*[18]

## Deer 8 [of 15] poems

a mountain hot spring;
  the face of a deer at the railing

山の温泉や欄に向へる鹿の面
*yama no yu ya ran ni mukaeru shika no tsura*

from within the privy I sense a deer;
  snorting

厠より鹿と覺しや鼻の息
*kawaya yori shika to oboshi ya hana no iki*

a temple gate;
  the moon resting on the antlers of a stag

山門や月に立たる鹿の角
*sanmon ya tsuki ni tachitaru shika no tsuno*

AUTUMN

sharp cry
    bounding off the boulder;
        the rump of a deer

ひいと鳴て岩を下るや鹿の尻
*hii to naite iwa o oriru ya shika no shiri*

at the shallows
    its neck lowered—
        a deer in moonlight

水淺く首を伏せけり月の鹿
*mizu asaku kubi o fusekeri tsuki no shika*

looking down
    on the mountain peak
        a lone deer

見下して尾上に鹿のひとりかな
*mioroshite onoe ni shika no hitori kana*

deer at eventide and deer at dayspring;
  how short my dreams

宵の鹿夜明の鹿や夢短か
*yoi no shika yoake no shika ya yume mijika*

daybreak;
  by the light of the fading moon
    a deer

曉や消ぬべき月に鹿あはれ
*akatsuki ya kenubeki tsuki ni shika aware*

overhead as I push through the pampas grass;
  autumn sky

押分くる芒の上や秋の空
*oshiwakuru susuki no ue ya aki no sora*

a single chrysanthemum petal in a tuanshi inkstone
  on the desk

端溪に菊一輪の机かな
*tankei ni kiku ichi rin no tsukue kana*

tormented by severe heartburn;
    chill autumn rains

酸多き胃を患ひてや秋の雨
*san ōki i o wazuraite ya aki no ame*

an ocean of dew surrounds my hermitage
    Confederate roses

露けさの庵を繞りて芙蓉かな
*tsuyukesa no iori o magurite fuyō kana*

returning home through the heavy dew;
    small lanterns

露けさの中に帰るや小提灯
*tsuyukesa no naka ni kaeru ya kochōchin*

the north window open
    wild geese against the moon

北窓は鎖さで居たり月の雁
*kita mado wa tozasa de itari tsuki no kari*

brushing against the mast
the moon-shadow of wild geese

帆柱をかすれて月の雁の影
*hobashira o kasurete tsuki no kari no kage*

through a gap in the hedge of a thatched hut
yellow chrysanthemums

草庵の垣にひまある黄菊かな
*sōan no kaki ni hima aru kigiku kana*

together with the grass
bellflowers pleached in the hedge

草共に桔梗を垣に結ひ込みぬ
*kusa tomo ni kikyō o kaki ni yuikominu*

white bellflowers by an old mortuary tablet
refreshing

白桔梗古き位牌にすがすがし
*shirogikyō furuki ihai ni sugasugashi*

*194*

poking through the holes in a grasscutter's basket
    bellflowers

草刈の籠の目を洩る桔梗かな
*kusakari no kago no me o moru kikyō kana*

the whine of fall mosquitoes has ceased
    my study

秋の蚊の鳴かずなりたる書齋かな
*aki no ka no nakazunaritaru shosai kana*

right before my eyes
    a dragonfly alit
        on the tip of my brush

まのあたり精霊来たり筆の先
*ma no atari shōryō kitari fude no saki*

a gelid morning;
    I cook two measures of rice by myself

朝寒や自ら炊ぐ飯二合
*asasamu ya mizukara kashigu meshi ni gō*

parting ways in the old capital;
a quail cries

手を分つ古き都や鶉泣く
*te o wakatsu furuki miyako ya uzura naku*

## In Xiongyuecheng

millet in the distance
people approaching the bath on the river bank

黍遠し河原の風呂へ渡る人
*kibi tōshi kawara no furo e wataru hito*[19]

through the grass and into the pines—
autumn wind

草盡きて松に入りけり秋の風
*kusa tsukite matsu ni irikeri aki no kaze*

looking up as my ears fill with a whip crack;
a night bright with stars

鞭鳴らす頭の上や星月夜
*muchi narasu atama no ue ya hoshizukiyo*

# AUTUMN

the cloudless autumn sky;
 a lone pine atop a mountain peak

秋晴や山の上なる一つ松
*akibare ya yama no ue naru hitotsu matsu*

a lone bamboo copse
 motionless;
  autumn village

動かざる一篁や秋の村
*ugokazaru hitotakamura ya aki no mura*

from the mouth of the "Copper Bull"
 late autumn storm

銅の牛の口より野分哉
*akagane no ushi no kuchi yori nowaki kana*[20]

the mosquito net hanger abruptly sways;
 early autumn morning

不圖揺るる蚊帳の釣手や今朝の秋
*futo yururu kaya no tsurite ya kesa no aki*

strains of a bamboo flute
an autumn diversion;
someone at the railing

尺八を秋のすさみや欄の人
*shakuhachi o aki no susami ya ran no hito*

---

**Autumn, fair. Lying here, looking at the sky. Shave.**[21]

clear autumn sky
a respite from my illness;
I will shave my beard

秋晴に病閒あるや髭を剃る
*akibare ni byōkan aru ya hige o soru*

---

the autumn sky has cleared to beryl
ax to a cedar

秋の空淺黃に澄めり杉に斧
*aki no sora asagi ni sumeri sugi no ono*

## AUTUMN

in my weakened state
    the chill night air closes in;
        the sound of rain

衰に夜寒逼るや雨の音
*otoroe ni yosamu semaru ya ame no oto*

blowing on skin and bones
    the storm winds of autumn on my ailing body

骨立を吹けば疾む身に野分かな
*kotsuritsu o fukeba yamu mi ni nowaki kana*

a day of illness
    again through a gap in the rattan blinds
        autumn butterfly

病む日又簾の隙より秋の蝶
*yamu hi mata sudare no suki yori aki no chō*

dragonfly dream;
    how many times to the tip of the piling?

蜻蛉の夢や幾度杭の先
*seirei no yume ya ikutabi kui no saki*

dragonfly;
    the ceaseless flash of its wings

蜻蛉や留り損ねて羽の光
*seirei ya tomarisokonete ha no hikari*

---

insects here and there on this night of illness;
    my heart is calm

虫遠近病む夜ぞ静なる心
*mushi ochikochi yamu yo zo shizuka naru kokoro*

---

I am thrilled to reënter the ranks of the living
    chrysanthemums in fall

生き返るわれ嬉しさよ菊の秋
*ikikaeru ware ureshisa yo kiku no aki*

---

perchance Noriyori's grave is getting wet
    autumn rainfall

範頼の墓濡るゝらん秋の雨
*Noriyori no haka nurururan aki no ame*[22]

## AUTUMN

my illness has abated
    clear autumn sky

静なる病に秋の空晴れたり
*shizuka naru yamai ni aki no sora haretari*

how strange
    looking at them upright;
        autumn mountains

竪に見て事珍らしや秋の山
*tate ni mite koto mezurashi ya aki no yama*

setting a lantern
    long the night in a well-lit room

ともし置いて室明き夜の長かな
*tomoshi oite heya akaki yo no nagaki kana*

enervated;
    autumn rice gruel for this wasted frame

力なや痩せたる吾に秋の粥
*chikara na ya yasetaru ware ni aki no kayu*

autumn mosquitoes;
  I wonder
    come daybreak will they bite me?

秋の蚊や我を螫さんと夜明方
*aki no ka ya ware o sasan to yoakegata*

---

the aroma of new rice stalks;
  the month changes
    yet I still feel ill

稲の香や月改まる病心地
*ina no ka ya tsuki aratamaru yamigokochi*

---

although I should return, I have not
  full moon in mid August

帰るべくて帰らぬ吾に月今宵
*kaerubekute kaeranu ware ni tsuki koyoi*

AUTUMN

I am restored
　　bit by bit
　　　　over the long nights

甦へる我は夜長に少しづゝ
*yomigaeru ware wa yonaga ni sukoshizutsu*

wagtails;
　　white guano on the branches of a small pine tree

鶺鴒や小松の枝に白き糞
*sekirei ya komatsu no eda ni shiroki fun*

over the cool roof tiles
　　birds flit to and fro

冷やかな瓦を鳥の遠近す
*hiyayaka na kawara o tori no ochikochi su*

coolness;
　　people sleeping calmly
　　　　the sound of water

冷かや人寐靜まり水の音
*hiyayaka ya hito neshizumari mizu no oto*

a gelid morning;
    the striking pain of fifty beats on a drum

朝寒や太鼓に痛き五十棒
*asasamu ya taiko ni itaki gojūbō*

useless legs
    a cart for the scarecrow

足腰の立たぬ案山子を車かな
*ashikoshi no tatanu kakashi o kuruma kana*

nothing but bones
    the scarecrow's floating world

骨許りになりて案山子の浮世かな
*hone bakari ni narite kakashi no ukiyo kana*

ill I came and ill I go
    I am a scarecrow

病んで來り病んで去る吾に案山子哉
*yandekitari yandesaru ware ni kakashi kana*

# AUTUMN

the rice ripens, the cured depart;
    a hot springs town

稲熟し人癒えて去るや温泉の村
*ine jukushi hito ietesaru ya deyu no mura*

---

against my renewed life
    the agelessness of autumn

新らしき命に秋の古きかな
*atarashiki inochi ni aki no furuki kana*

---

I now recall—
    there have already been several nights of crickets

思ひけり既に幾夜の蟋蟀
*omoikeri sudeni ikuyo no kirigirisu*

---

dawn;
    in a dream
        a faint moon

暁や夢のこなたに淡き月
*akatsuki ya yume no konata ni awaki tsuki*

calling pleasantly to mind a *kemari* ball
 chrysanthemum shadow

嬉しく思ふ蹴鞠の如き菊の影
*ureshiku omou kemari no gotoki kiku no kage*

how keenly I feel it
 the length of a night of lanterns

つくづくと行燈の夜の長さかな
*tsukuzuku to andon no yo no nagaki kana*

a clump of silver pampas grass
 the strength of the wind

一叢の薄に風の強き哉
*hitomura no susuki ni kaze no tsuyoki kana*

a lone persimmon
 lingering on the branch
 a crow

柿一つ枝に殘りて烏哉
*kaki hitotsu eda ni nokorite karasu kana*

AUTUMN

a night when but one came—
 a moonlit goose

たゞ一羽來る夜ありけり月の雁
*tada ichiwa kuru yo arikeri tsuki no kari*

dipping water from the well
 white chrysanthemums in the early morning

井戸の水汲む白菊の晨哉
*ido no mizu kumu shiragiku no ashita kana*

with late October comes the rain;
 ever since last night

三日の菊雨と變るや昨夕より
*mikka no kiku ame to kawaru ya yūbe yori*

white and yellow chrysanthemums blooming
 Japan

白菊と黄菊と咲いて日本かな
*shiragiku to kigiku to saite Nihon kana*

fragrant chrysanthemums ;
    several pots resting on the southern verandah

菊の香や幾鉢置いて南縁
*kiku no ka ya iku hachi oite minami en*

———

since receiving a Zōtaku bamboo painting
    dew drapes my hermitage

藏澤の竹を得てより露の庵
*Zōtaku no take o ete yori tsuyu no an*[23]

———

in illness
    I dreamt
        flood waters from the River of Heaven

病んで夢む天の川より出水かな
*yande yumemu amanogawa yori demizu kana*

———

a sea of dew about the village
    my illness in abeyance

露けさの里にて靜かなる病
*tsuyukesa no sato nite shizuka naru yamai*

# AUTUMN

a gelid morning;
    these living bones unmoving

朝寒や生きたる骨を動かさず
*asasamu ya ikitaru hone o ugokasazu*

on the ornamental post cap atop the balustrade
    a single dragonfly

勾欄の擬寶珠に一つ蜻蛉哉
*kōran no giboshi ni hitotsu tonbo kana*

taking out a letter box
    cool to the touch
        gold lacquer

冷かな文箱差出す蒔繪かな
*hiyayaka na fubako sashidasu makie kana*

# SŌSEKI NATSUME'S COLLECTED HAIKU

**While I was ill, Roseki paid me a visit, but I did not meet with him, so I sent him this poem afterwards.**

you took your leave while I slept—
    early autumn morning

起きぬ間に露石去にけり今朝の秋
*okinu ma ni Roseki inikeri kesa no aki*[24]

bats every night;
    thin rice gruel

蝙蝠の宵々毎や薄き粥
*kōmori no yoi yoi goto ya usuki kayu*

**In a corner hospital room on the third floor**

so close the lightning
    sleep comes uneasily

稲妻に近くて眠安からず
*inazuma ni chikakute nemuri yasukarazu*

across the incision
    a cool breeze from the privy hole

切口に冷やかな風の厠より
*kirikuchi ni hiyayaka na kaze no kawaya yori*[25]

the hair at my temples flutters in the mirror
    early autumn morning

鬢の影鏡にそよと今朝の秋
*bin no kage kagami ni soyo to kesa no aki*

## Walls

only the spindle falls from the hanging scroll
    an autumn wall

懸物の軸だけ落ちて壁の秋
*kakemono no jiku dake ochite kabe no aki*

## Walls

even the foraging mice;
    back into their holes they retreat from the night chill

鼠もや出ると夜寒に壁の穴
*nezumi mo ya deru to yosamu ni kabe no ana*

autumn wind;
    the rump of a cow heading to slaughter

秋風や屠られに行く牛の尻
*akikaze ya hofurare ni yuku ushi no shiri*

I go alone to the far end of a field;
    autumn sky

我一人行く野の末や秋の空
*ware hitori yuku no no sue ya aki no sora*

a drop of *sake* at the bottom of the flask
    cold autumn night

酒少し徳利の底に夜寒哉
*sake sukoshi tokuri no soko ni yosamu kana*

unable to sleep
    a lamp at night;
        autumn rain

眠らざる夜半の灯や秋の雨
*nemurazaru yowa no akari ya aki no ame*

---

**For my dog**

buried
    unable to hear the autumn wind

秋風の聞えぬ土に埋めてやりぬ
*akikaze no kikoenu tsuchi ni umeteyarinu*

---

a lone bamboo with four or five leaves
    winter draws nigh

竹一本葉四五枚に冬近し
*take ippon ha shi-gomai ni fuyu chikashi*

SŌSEKI NATSUME'S COLLECTED HAIKU

chrysanthemums
   visible through the glass door

菊の花硝子戸越に見ゆる哉
*kiku no hana garasudogoshi ni miyuru kana*

---

autumn has come;
   one volume left to read

秋立つや一巻の書の讀み殘し
*akitatsu ya ikkan no sho no yominokoshi*

---

penning tributes to bush clover and ferns
   sitting in a circle of moonlight

萩と歯朶に贅書く月の團居哉
*hagi to shida ni san kaku tsuki no madoi kana*

---

early fall day
   the focused eyes of a hunting cat

秋立つ日猫の蚤取眼かな
*akitatsu hi neko no nomitori manako kana*

*214*

## What of the gourd?

will the gourd rattle or not?
autumn winds

瓢箪は鳴るか鳴らぬか秋の風
*hyōtan wa naru ka naranu ka aki no kaze*

---

a clump of pampas grass sways
has autumn arrived?

ひとむらの芒動いて立つ秋か
*hitomura no susuki ugoite tatsuaki ka*

---

how like a tiger is my cat
autumn winds

吾猫も虎にやならん秋の風
*waga neko mo tora ni ya naran aki no kaze*

# Winter

冬

an invalid leaves the foot-warming table
   snowfall viewing

病む人の巨燵離れて雪見かな
*yamu hito no kotatsu hanarete yukimi kana*

---

a raging winter gale;
   Lake Biwa

驀地に凩吹くや鳰の湖
*mashigura ni kogarashi fuku ya Nionoumi*

---

lifted by the wind
   surmounting the pagoda;
     fallen leaves

吹き上げて塔より上の落葉かな
*fukiagete tō yori ue no ochiba kana*

o're the five-storied pagoda
    lifted by the wind
        fallen leaves

五重の塔吹き上げられて落葉かな
*gojū no tō fukiagerarete ochiba kana*

ceaselessly to the waterfall basin they come
    fallen leaves

瀧壺に寄りもつかれぬ落葉かな
*takitsubo ni yori mo tsukarenu ochiba kana*

halfway down
    the waterfall blows them back
        fallen leaves

半途より瀧吹き返す落葉かな
*hanto yori taki fukikaesu ochiba kana*

cataracts large and small
near the top, near the bottom
leaves in autumn hues

男瀧女瀧上よ下よと木の葉かな
*odaki medaki ue yo shita yo to konoha kana*

dancing suddenly at the grotto's mouth
leaves in autumn hues

洞門に颯と舞ひ込む木の葉かな
*dōmon ni satto maikomu konoha kana*

winter mountains
even if people passed, I would not have seen them

冬の山人通ふとも見えざりき
*fuyu no yama hito kayō to mo miezariki*

in a withering wind a whale blows
Hirado

凩に鯨潮吹く平戸かな
*kogarashi ni kujira shio fuku Hirado kana*

sporadic drizzle;
a feral kitten asleep atop the sutras

時雨るゝや泥猫眠る經の上
*shigururu ya doraneko nemuru kyō no ue*

maple leaves scatter
crinkling

紅葉散るちりゝちりゝとちゞくれて
*momiji chiru chiriri chiriri to chijikurete*

Kusayama range
mountains atop mountains
the first month of winter

草山の重なり合へる小春哉
*Kusayama no kasanariaeru koharu kana*

intermittent rain;
ambient sound on the temple roof

時雨るゝや聞としもなく寺の屋根
*shigururu ya kiku to shi mo naku tera no yane*

sporadic drizzle;
   the smoke from frying tofu
      a bamboo curtain

時雨るゝや油揚烟る繩簾
*shigururu ya aburage keburu nawasudare*

---

Benkei
   in the cold moonlight on Gojō Bridge

辨慶に五條の月の寒さ哉
*Benkei ni gojō no tsuki no samusa kana*[1]

---

a withering wind;
   the waterfall turns back whence it came

凩や瀧に當つて引き返す
*kogarashi ya taki ni atatte hikikaesu*

---

you, blind jongleur, wait
   shall I lend you a wrapping cloth?
      hail is falling

待て座頭風呂敷かさん霰ふる
*mate zatō furoshiki kasan arare furu*

the thirty-six peaks vying with one another
    sporadic drizzle

三十六峰我も我もと時雨けり
*sanjūroppō ware mo ware mo shigurekeri*[2]

---

first rain of late fall
    to the five main temples go the visiting hordes

初時雨五山の交る交る哉
*hatsushigure gozan no kawarugawaru kana*

---

**Expressing my desire for you to come visit me as I lie here,
ill with the excesses of debauchery**

at autumn's gloaming
    a mendicant priest reaches the barrier gate

秋の暮關所へかゝる虚無僧あり
*aki no kure sekisho e kakaru komusō ari*

WINTER

I have taken ill
  arrange the camellia there, by my pillow

我病めり山茶花活けよ枕元
*ware yameri sazanka ikeyo makuramoto*

a heavy snowstorm;
  a brave youth bags a brown bear and heads home

大雪や壮夫羆を獲て帰る
*ōyuki ya sōfu higuma o ete kaeru*

while I can see a single star, sleep eludes me
  this frosty night

星一つ見えて寐られぬ霜夜哉
*hoshi hitotsu miete nerarenu shimoyo kana*

frost-marked morning
  ugh! my pocket watch has stopped

霜の朝袂時計のとまりけり
*shimo no asa tamotodokei tomarikeri*

a tree-withering wind now?
    no leaves to scatter even as it blows

木枯の今や吹くとも散る葉なし
*kogarashi no ima ya fuku tomo chiru ha nashi*

the gripes sets in
    the cold on my restless butt

疝氣持臀安からぬ寒哉
*senkimochi shiri yasukaranu samusa kana*

the verdant bamboo
    luxuriant
        long falls the snow

綠竹の猗々たり霏々と雪が降る
*ryokuchiku no iitari hihi to yuki ga furu*

the season's first snow;
    from the temple kitchen
        sounds of tenderizing duck

初雪や庫裏は眞鴨をたゝく音
*hatsuyuki ya kuri wa magamo o tataku oto*

# WINTER

a hint of cold in the air
    the limit of my thoughts

何となく寒いと我は思ふのみ
*nantonaku samui to ware wa omou nomi*

---

if I pass away
    to whom should I pass on my paper garments?

我死なば紙衣を誰に譲るべき
*ware shinaba kamiko o dare ni yuzurubeki*[3]

---

the season's first snow;
    into the lane comes the fermented-soybean seller

初雪や小路へ入る納豆賣
*hatsuyuki ya komichi e hairu natto-uri*

---

banging on the purifying trough
    fragmented ice

御手洗を敲いて砕く氷かな
*mitarashi o tataite kudaku kōri kana*

old quilted garments
　　thoroughly lousy with lice
　　　first month of winter

古綿衣虱の多き小春哉
*kowataginu shirami no ōki koharu kana*

just as the withered willow turned green again
　　a dear young woman passed on

枯柳緑なる頃妹逝けり
*kareyanagi midori naru koro imo yukeri*

a young girl
　　learning *haiku*
　　　first month of winter

女の子發句を習ふ小春哉
*onna no ko hokku o narau koharu kana*

there should also be a tom in heat
　　blossoms out of season

戀をする猫もあるべし歸花
*koi o suru neko mo arubeshi kaeribana*

# WINTER

vegetable rice gruel prepared with affection;
   late-fall rain at night

懇ろに雑炊たくや小夜時雨
*nengoro ni zōsui taku ya sayoshigure*

winter's desolation;
   Ōbakuji temple bathed in the setting sun

冬枯や夕陽多き黄檗寺
*fuyugare ya sekiyō ōki Ōbakuji*

time and time again a horse whinnies
   blizzard

あまた度馬の嘶く吹雪哉
*amata tabi uma no inanaku fubuki kana*

a tempest
   a hawk veers unexpectedly o'er a desolate field

嵐して鷹のそれたる枯野哉
*arashi shite taka no soretaru kareno kana*

a ferocious hawk takes down a crane;
    snowy plain

あら鷹の鶴蹴落すや雪の原
*ara taka no tsuru keotosu ya yuki no hara*

in a bamboo thicket
    pheasant cries
        falconry

竹藪に雉子鳴き立つる鷹野哉
*takeyabu ni kiji nakitatsuru takano kana*

by a small fire
    lo! he has fallen asleep—
        night weir watchman

焚火して居眠りけりな網代守
*takibi shite inemurikeri na ajiromori*

pufferfish soup;
    there are nights when I see dreams of my death

河豚汁や死んだ夢見る夜もあり
*fugujiru ya shinda yume miru yoru mo ari*

## Mourning

cold evening sun
    ragged violet clouds

夕日寒く紫の雲崩れけり
*yūhi samuku murasaki no kumo kuzurekeri*

---

## Mourning

a corpse
    a hot water bottle grown totally cold

亡骸に冷え盡したる煖甫哉
*nakigara ni hietsukushitaru tanpo kana*

---

rest assured;
    eating game for one night also relieves the gripes

落付や疝氣も一夜藥喰
*ochitsuku ya senki mo hitoyo kusurigui*

riverside fish market;
　　rinsing salted salmon
　　　the sound of water

魚河岸や乾鮭洗ふ水の音
*uogashi ya karazake arau mizu no oto*

the bath has cooled
　　I make to get out but can't
　　　my god it's cold

温泉をぬるみ出るに出られぬ寒さ哉
*yu o nurumi deru ni derarenu samusa kana*

holed up in winter
　　even the kitten is safe and fed

冬籠り小猫も無事で罷りある
*fuyugomori koneko mo buji de makari aru*

over two miles on the bank and nary an evergreen;
　　barren winter trees

土堤一里常盤木もなしに冬木立
*dote ichi ri tokiwagi mo nashi ni fuyukodachi*

WINTER

the clear winter moon;
    by the edge of a dry fosse
        an udon seller

寒月やから堀端のうどん賣
*kangetsu ya kara horibata no udon uri*

in my sleep
    I hear a slap, slap, slap
        pounding out new year's rice cakes

寐て聞くやぺたりぺたりと餅の音
*nete kiku ya petari petari to mochi no oto*

brimming with vigor
    the jostling crowds of Edo's year-end marketplace

勢ひやひしめく江戸の年の市
*ikioi ya hishimeku Edo no toshi no ichi*

my age at year's end;
    ensuring each moment counts
        the sound of water

行年や刹那を急ぐ水の音
*yuku toshi ya setsuna o isogu mizu no oto*

cold bamboo grass in the mountain's shadow
    the sound of water

山陰に熊笹寒し水の音
*yamakage ni kumazasa samushi mizu no oto*

early winter;
    the sound of a hatchet cutting bamboo in the mountains

初冬や竹切る山の鉈の音
*hatsufuyu ya take kiru yama no nata no oto*

winter withering on one patch of the mountains
    verdant bamboo

冬枯れて山の一角竹青し
*fuyu karete yama no ikkaku take aoshi*

WINTER

kudzu crawls up the side of the charcoal kiln
   even as it withers

炭竈に葛這ひ上る枯れながら
*sumigama ni kuzu hainoboru karenagara*

from the east and west
   from the south and north
      a fearsome blizzard

東西南北より吹雪哉
*higashi nishi minami kita yori fubuki kana*

nestling the wooden rice tub under the bed quilts
   a widow

飯櫃を蒲團につゝむ孀哉
*meshibitsu o futon ni tsutsumu yamome kana*

accepting a steamed yam in his head scarf
   the head priest

煨芋を頭巾に受くる和尚哉
*yakiimo o zukin ni ukuru oshō kana*

looking so joyous under a down quilt
    your sleeping countenance

毛蒲團に君は目出度寐顔かな
*kebuton ni kimi wa medataku /negao kana*

a snowy day;
    the *Tosa Diary* slips off the *kotstsu*

雪の日や火燵をすべる土佐日記
*yuki no hi ya kotatsu o suberu Tosa nikki*

"coming. coming."
    extracting oneself to go greet the guests
        *kotatsu*

應々と取次に出ぬ火燵哉
*ōō to toritsugi ni denu kotatsu kana*

into the banked fire fell mouse turds

埋火に鼠の糞の落ちにけり
*uzumibi ni nezumi no fun no ochinikeri*

at daybreak the banked fire finally dies
   how cold it is

曉の埋火消ゆる寒さ哉
*akatsuki no uzumibi kiyuru samusa kana*

chrysanthemums wither in a copper kettle
   the cold of night

銅瓶に菊枯るゝ夜の寒哉
*dōbin ni kiku karuru yo no samusa kana*

by and by this chill becomes fearsome
   a Seto brazier

冷たくてやがて恐ろし瀬戸火鉢
*tsumetakute yagate osoroshi seto hibachi*[4]

silently smoothing the ash in the brazier

黙然と火鉢の灰をならしけり
*mokunen to hibachi no hai o narashikeri*

a tea tasting
    yikes! what an uncouth boor
        letting loose a fart

口切にこはけしからぬ放屁哉
*kuchikiri ni ko wa keshikaranu hōhi kana*

withered as they are
    frozen vines on a monstrous boulder

枯ながら蔦の氷れる岩哉
*karenagara tsuta no kōreru iwao kana*

on a bony horse
    a dangerous mountain path
        so icy

痩馬に山路危き氷哉
*yaseuma ni yamaji ayōki kōri kana*

a single water droplet on the hairs of the brush
    frozen solid

筆の毛の水一滴を氷りけり
*fude no ke no mizu itteki o kōrikeri*

*236*

WINTER

the narcissus leaves indifferent though they are
    so icy

水仙の葉はつれなくも氷哉
*suisen no ha wa tsurenaku mo kōri kana*

---

the bridge has rotted
    the winter river is dry
        moonlit night

橋朽ちて冬川枯るゝ月夜哉
*hashi kuchite fuyukawa karuru tsukiyo kana*

---

**At the grave of Noriyori**

a withering wind;
    a young man's grave pelted with falling pine needles

凩や冠者の墓撲つ落松葉
*kogarashi ya kaja no haka utsu ochimatsuba*[5]

## SŌSEKI NATSUME'S COLLECTED HAIKU

a mountain temple;
  the winter sun lingers above the ocean

山寺や冬の日殘る海の上
*yamadera ya fuyu no hi nokoru umi no ue*

a snake emerges from its burrow;
  first month of winter

穴蛇の穴を出でたる小春哉
*anahebi no ana o idetaru koharu kana*

deeply piled snow;
  bloodstains tapering off at the tiger's lair

積雪や血痕絶えて虎の穴
*sekisetsu ya kekkon taete tora no ana*

how industrious;
  a priest beats an iron gong at night while hail falls

いそがしや霰ふる夜の鉢叩
*isogashi ya arare furu yo no hachitataki*

*238*

the year has grown old;
    sitting knee to knee
        we meet

行く年や膝と膝とをつき合せ
*yuku toshi ya hiza to hiza to o tsukiawase*

my head hung low
    grasping my knees
        how cold it is

うつむいて膝にだきつく寒哉
*utsumuite hiza ni dakitsuku samusa kana*

departing down the lantern-bedecked hall
    how cold it is

雪洞の廊下をさがる寒さ哉
*bonbori no rōka o sagaru samusa kana*

the water has dried up leaving only wheel ruts;
    winter river

水涸れて轍のあとや冬の川
*mizu karete wadachi no ato ya fuyu no kawa*

SŌSEKI NATSUME'S COLLECTED HAIKU

a house in the valley
    strains of a bamboo flute in sporadic rain

谷の家竹法螺の音に時雨けり
*tani no ie takebora no ne ni shigurekeri*

the snowfall clears
    the susurration of rebounding bamboo

雪霽たり竹婆娑々々と跳返る
*yuki haretari take basabasa to tobikaeru*

clear blue waters
    accumulated snow atop an earthen-paved bridge

水青し土橋の上に積る雪
*mizu aoshi dobashi no ue ni tsumoru yuki*

leaving after the viewing
    sated with early plum blossoms

見て行くやつばらつばらに寒の梅
*mite yuku ya tsubaratsubara ni kan no ume*

*240*

# WINTER

whither silence?
　snow snapping the bamboo makes sleeping difficult

靜かさは竹折る雪に寐かねたり
*shizukasa wa take oru yuki ni nekanetari*


on Musashino plain
　falling horizontally
　　winter rain

武蔵野を横に降る也冬の雨
*Musashino o yoko ni furunari fuyu no ame*


shall I venture forth to beard the lion in his den?
　a snowy morning

いざや我虎穴に入らん雪の朝
*izaya ware koketsu ni iran yuki no asa*


a single dwelling quietly buried beneath the snow

一つ家のひそかに雪に埋れけり
*hitotsuya no hisoka ni yuki ni umorekeri*

dismounting my horse
there stands a single signboard—
winter rain

下馬札の一つ立ちけり冬の雨
*geba fuda no hitotsu tachikeri fuyu no ame*

inadvisable thought it be
I look back
winter blizzard

まさなくも後ろを見する吹雪哉
*masanaku mo ushiro o misuru fubuki kana*

stone washbasin
scattered camellia blossoms frozen fast

つくばいに散る山茶花の氷りけり
*tsukubai ni chiru sazanka no kōrikeri*

a crow takes flight
against the evening sun sway winter trees

烏飛んで夕日に動く冬木かな
*karasu tonde yūhi ni ugoku fuyuki kana*

# WINTER

erecting a stage to fête the Big Dipper;
    hoarfrost spears atop the ground

壇築て北斗祭るや剣の霜
*dan tsukite hokuto matsuru ya ken no shimo*

---

blowing in through the cloisters
    ocean blizzard

廻廊に吹きこむ海の吹雪かな
*kairō ni fukikomu umi no fubuki kana*

---

at the gate
    willows standing five in a row
        branches weeping down

門柳五本並んで枝垂れけり
*kadoyanagi gohon narande shitarekeri*

---

with nary a sound he inflates his belly
    pufferfish

物言はで腹ふくれたる河豚かな
*monoiwade hara fukuretaru fukuto kana*

early winter;
the path to enlightenment is yet impassable

初冬や向上の一路未だ開かず
*hatsufuyu ya kōjō no ichiro imada akazu*

an early winter *koto*
the discordant strains of tuning up

初冬の琴面白の音じめ哉
*hatsufuyu no koto omoshiro no nejime kana*

a withering wind
blows the eventide sun down into the sea

凩や海に夕日を吹き落す
*kogarashi ya umi ni yūhi o fukiotosu*

late autumn rain on the bamboo I planted
listening at night

吾栽し竹に時雨を聴く夜哉
*waga ueshi take ni shigure o kiku yo kana*

# WINTER

worthy of a poem
  Rashōmon in a late autumn rain

謠ふべき程は時雨つ羅生門
*utaubeki hodo wa shiguretsu Rashōmon*

moving behind a silver folding screen
  narcissus blossoms

銀屛を後ろにしたり水仙花
*ginbyō o ushiro ni shitari suisenka*

pine trees twisted by the withering winds
  atop a hill

凩の松はねぢれつ岡の上
*kogarashi no matsu wa nejiretsu oka no ue*

walking the fields
  I suffer in the cold wind

野を行けば寒がる吾を風が吹く
*no o yukeba samugaru ware o kaze ga fuku*

wielding a whip
   riding a horse into a withering wind

策つて凩の中に馬のり入るゝ
*muchiutte kogarashi no naka uma no noriiruru*

---

rice porridge;
   in a well-loved bowl
      hunkered down for winter

雑炊や古き茶椀に冬籠
*zōsui ya furuki chawan ni fuyugomori*

---

is that polyphony a hen and her chicks?
   quails crying to the south

重なるは親子か南に鳴く鶉
*kasanaru wa oyako ka minami ni naku uzura*

---

the passing year sees the rent go up
   Kōjimachi

行年を家賃上げたり麹町
*yukutoshi o yachin agetari kōjimachi*[6]

WINTER

year's end finds my wife preparing a meal—
    steamed rice with millet

行年を妻炊ぎけり粟の飯
*yukutoshi o tsuma kashigikeri awa no meshi*

drunk
    pounding at the gate;
        December moonlight

酔て叩く門や師走の月の影
*yotte tataku mon ya shiwasu no tsuki no kage*

a plenteous heap
    doubtless some will have gone bad
        clementines

累々と徳孤ならずの蜜柑哉
*ruirui to toku ko narazu no mikan kana*

raking smooth the ashes
    leaves appear

かきならす灰の中より木の葉哉
*kakinarasu hai no naka yori konoha kana*

*247*

SŌSEKI NATSUME'S COLLECTED HAIKU

following the train
the smoke crawls languidly
o'er desolate fields

汽車を逐て煙這行枯野哉
*kisha o otte kemuri haiyuku kareno kana*

greetings;
hail tumbles from the topknot

挨拶や髷の中より出る霰
*aisatsu ya mage no naka yori deru arare*

huddled together, wandering samurai take flight
a desolate field

かたまつて野武士落行枯野哉
*katamatte nobushi ochiyuku kareno kana*

*248*

WINTER

## Wei Shuzi *The Legend of the Great Iron Hammer*

the shooting stars;
    across a desolate field move beech tree shadows

星飛ぶや枯野に動く椎の影
*hoshi tobu ya kareno ni ugoku shii no kage*[7]


a lone bird blown backwards
    o'er a desolate field

鳥一つ吹き返さるゝ枯野かな
*tori hitotsu fukikaesaruru kareno kana*


with a rustle the dead leaves of the chestnut fall;
    the shriek of a shrike

さらさらと栗の落葉や鵙の聲
*sarasara to kuri no ochiba ya mozu no koe*

SŌSEKI NATSUME'S COLLECTED HAIKU

abandoned house;
    ice on the stone washbasin
        silverleaf blossoms

空家やつくばひ氷る石蕗の花
*akiie ya tsukubai kōru tsuwa no hana*

the sound of a guest slipping on the stepping stones
    silverleaf blossoms

飛石に客すべる音す石蕗の花
*tobiishi ni kyaku suberu otosu tsuwa no hana*

I awake and look about
    my guest is sound asleep—
        beside the hearth

覺めて見れば客眠りけり爐のわきに
*samete mireba kyaku nemurikeri ro no waki ni*

*250*

WINTER

how wonderful!
emerging from the snow
a sago palm

面白し雪の中より出る蘇鉄
*omoshiroshi yuki no naka yori deru sotetsu*

priest and layman
face to face
a wooden brazier

僧俗の差し向ひたる火桶哉
*sōzoku no sashimukaitaru hioke kana*

tales told by burns and scratches;
agèd paulownia brazier

物語る手創や古りし桐火桶
*monogataru tekizu ya furishi kiri hioke*

*251*

enriching the house
   sunlight pours through the windows in winter's first month

家富んで窓に小春の日陰かな
*ie tonde mado ni koharu no hikage kana*

the white flag of the Minamoto clan;
   a snow-clad stand of trees at Kiso

白旗の源氏や木曾の冬木立
*shirahata no Genji ya Kiso no fuyukodachi*

sporadic drizzle bedeviled the Taira clan
   at Goka-no-shō

時雨るゝは平家につらし五家荘
*shigururu wa Heike ni tsurashi gokanoshō*[8]

beneath the hall, a deep pool
   within the pool, light
     the winter moon

堂下潭あり潭裏影あり冬の月
*dōka tan ari tanri kage ari fuyu no tsuki*

opening the door
   astonishment
      snowy morning

戸を開けて驚く雪の晨かな
*to o akete odoroku yuki no ashita kana*

---

a doctor unburdened by patients edits poems
   holed up for winter

醫はやらず歌など撰し冬籠
*i wa yarazu uta nado senshi fuyugomori*

---

a lit candle
   a charcoal-ink-drawn daruma
      deep cold

燭つきつ墨繪の達磨寒氣なる
*shaku tsukitsu sumie no daruma kanki naru*

extinguishing the candle as dawn draws nigh
last night of the year

燭きつて曉ちかし大晦日
*shaku kitsute akatsuki chikashi ōmisoka*

the *sake* is bitter, the bedding is thin
sleepless night

酒苦く蒲團薄くて寝られぬ夜
*sake nigaku futon usukute nerarenu yo*

across the ages
sea cucumber
bloodless when sliced

古往今來切つて血の出ぬ海鼠かな
*koōkonrai kitte chi no denu namako kana*

## WINTER

### Swords

cold springtime
   suspended on a grave
      the youngest child's sword

春寒し墓に懸けたる季子の劍
*haru samushi haka ni kaketaru kishi no ken*

### Swords

a gelid sword
   open the door
      it's Fan Kuai

劍寒し闥を排して樊噲が
*ken samushi tatsu o haishite Han Kai ga*[9]

two or three camellia petals scattered on the floor

二三片山茶花散りぬ床の上
*ni san hen sazanka chirinu yuka no ue*

first rain of late fall
   my chronic complaint
      the gripes

初時雨吾に持病の疝氣あり
*hatsushigure ware ni jibyō no senki ari*

returning to lanterns at the mountain's foot
   late fall rain

提灯の根岸に歸る時雨かな
*chōchin no negishi ni kaeru shigure kana*

into the bamboo grass dives a rabbit
   hail

熊笹に兎飛び込む霰哉
*kumazasa ni usagi tobikomu arare kana*

ill
   confined two days to a portable brazier

病あり二日を籠る置炬燵
*yamai ari futsuka o komoru okigotatsu*

year's end;
    the cat curled up upon my lap

行く年や猫うづくまる膝の上
*yukutoshi ya neko uzukumaru hiza no ue*

---

I make to burn them
    yet, mixed in with the dried leaves
        hail

焚かんとす枯葉にまじる霰哉
*takan to su kareha ni majiru arare kana*

---

I step out of the house into the December rain in my raincoat

家を出て師走の雨に合羽哉
*ie o dete shiwasu no ame ni kappa kana*

---

at what are they pecking?
    a murder of crows in a winter field

何をつゝき鴉あつまる冬の畠
*nani o tsutsuki karasu atsumaru fuyu no hata*

SŌSEKI NATSUME'S COLLECTED HAIKU

at the hotspring gate
 ripe December persimmons

温泉の門に師走の熟柿かな
*onsen no mon ni shiwasu no jukushi kana*

you wish to journey on
 yet I dawdle at the inn
  year's end draws nigh

旅にして申譯なく暮るゝ年
*tabi ni shite mōshiwakenaku kururu toshi*

a withering wind there in the offing
 Ariake Sea

凩の沖へとあるゝ筑紫潟
*kogarashi no oki e to aruru Tsukushigata*

the ashen sky hanging low
 a barren plain

灰色の空低れかゝる枯野哉
*haiiro no sora tarekakaru kareno kana*

WINTER

crossing a barren field without a lantern
how cold it is

無提灯で枯野を通る寒哉
*muchōchin de kareno o tōru samusa kana*

---

withered pampas grass
bending northward waving in the wind

枯芒北に向つて靡きけり
*karesusuki kita ni mukatte nabikikeri*

---

gazing into the distance
smoke rising from a barren field

遠く見る枯野の中の烟かな
*tōku miru kareno no naka no kemuri kana*

---

in the bleak of winter;
a badger hung from the eaves

冬ざれや貉をつるす軒の下
*fuyuzare ya mujina o tsurusu noki no shita*

## At Rakanji Temple

a withering wind;
   clinging to the boulders along Rakanji Temple lane

凩や岩に取りつく羅漢路
*kogarashi ya iwa ni toritsuku Rakan michi*

---

## At Rakanji Temple

the clouds themselves ought to freeze to the hanging bell
   soaring mountains

釣鐘に雲氷るべく山高し
*tsurigane ni kumo kōrubeku yama takashi*

---

## At Rakanji Temple

at the precipice
   the cold winter wind strikes
      howling

絶壁に木枯あたるひゞきかな
*zeppeki ni kogarashi ataru hibiki kana*

# WINTER

## Overnighting at a place called Kuchinohayashi

too short, so I pile on blankets
    bedding

短かくて毛布つぎ足す蒲團かな
*mijikakute mōfu tsukitasu futon kana*

## At Yabakei Gorge

encountering a hooded hunter
    a deep cwm

頭巾着たる獵師に逢ひぬ谷深み
*zukin kitaru ryōshi ni ainu tani fukami*

## At Yabakei Gorge

men sending winter trees downriver
    how like macaques they appear

冬木流す人は猿の如くなり
*fuyuki nagasu hito wa mashira no gotoku nari*

## At Yabakei Gorge

the rocky mountain blown by a withering winter wind
    stripped naked

石の山凩に吹かれ裸なり
*ishi no yama kogarashi ni fukare hadaka nari*

---

## As if the moutains had been washed clean

withering winds blew
    not even pines grew

凩の吹くべき松も生えざりき
*kogarashi no fukubeki matsu mo haezariki*

---

year by year;
    mountains, sharpened by wild withering winds

年々や凩吹て尖る山
*toshidoshi ya kogarashi fuite togaru yama*

peaks honed by withering winds
    veritable swords

凩の峯は剣の如くなり
*kogarashi no mine wa tsurugi no gotoku nari*

the crunching of ice with each footstep—
    a glyn footpath

ばりばりと氷踏みけり谷の道
*baribari to kōri fumikeri tani no michi*

**Passing Kakisaka in the gorge**

along the wayside
    an ice-encrusted bamboo broom

道端や氷りつきたる高箒
*michibata ya kōri tsukitaru takabōki*

## Lodging at Morizane hot springs

curled up under the bedquilts;
    the whole night through

せぐゝまる蒲團の中や夜もすがら
*segukumaru futon no naka ya yo mo sugara*

thin bedquilts
    rubbing my benumbed, hairy shins

薄蒲團なえし毛脛を擦りけり
*usubuton naeshi kezune o kosurikeri*

## Crossing the pass and descending into Hita, Bungo

snow fluttering at the pass
    clinging to a raincoat

雪ちらちら峠にかゝる合羽かな
*yuki chirachira tōge ni kakaru kappa kana*

though I brush it off time and again
  snow on my sleeves

拂へども拂へどもわが袖の雪
*haraedomo haraedomo waga sode no yuki*

at the tunnel entrance
  a monstrous icicle

隧道の口に大なる氷柱かな
*zuidō no kuchi ni dai naru tsurara kana*

at the base of the swirling snowfall
  Hita village

吹きまくる雪の下なり日田の町
*fukimakuru yuki no shita nari Hita no machi*

the back of a horse laden with coal
  mottled by falling snow

炭を積む馬の脊に降る雪まだら
*sumi o tsumu uma no se ni furu yuki madara*

# SŌSEKI NATSUME'S COLLECTED HAIKU

**After being kicked by a horse and collapsing in the snow
as I was descending from the pass**

give it but a moment and I shall rise again
    blizzard

漸くに又起きあがる吹雪かな
*yōyaku ni mata okiagaru fubuki kana*

or'e the rapids hail blows
    dwarf bamboo

奔湍に霰ふり込む根笹かな
*hontan ni arare furikomu nezasa kana*

"it's seven miles, yet", comes the reply from up front
    blizzard

棒鼻より三里と答ふ吹雪哉
*bōbana yori sanri to kotau fubuki kana*

WINTER

## Lodging at Yoshii

listening with nostalgia under the quilt;
    horse harness bells

なつかしむ衾に聞くや馬の鈴
*natsukashimu fusuma ni kiku ya uma no suzu*

pounding rice cakes;
    Venus at dawn shimmering on the mallet head

餅搗や明星光る杵の先
*mochitsuki ya myōjō hikaru kine no saki*

not even old clothes to dye anew
    the year fades to dusk

染め直す古服もなし年の暮
*somenaosu furufuku mo nashi toshi no kure*

my fussy mother-in law is in fine health
    the year fades to dusk

やかましき姑健なり年の暮
*yakamashiki shūto ken nari toshi no kure*

## SŌSEKI NATSUME'S COLLECTED HAIKU

my nickel-plated watch has stopped
   the cold dead of night

ニッケルの時計とまりぬ寒き夜半
*nikkeru no tokei tomarinu samuki yowa*

---

senility
   that we term the cowl of old age

耄碌と名のつく老の頭巾かな
*mōroku to na no tsuku oi no zukin kana*

---

standing interminably
   stamping my feet
     how cold it is

立ん坊の地団太を踏む寒かな
*tachinbo no jidanda o fumu samusa kana*

---

when we move closer
   the Seto-ware brazier has gone cold

寄り添へば冷たき瀬戸の火鉢かな
*yorisoeba tsumetaki Seto no hibachi kana*

*268*

sporadic drizzle;
    a rotting step in a leaky temple

時雨るゝや足場朽ちたる堂の漏
*shigururu ya ashiba kuchitaru dō no mori*

banking the charcoal briquettes as skillfully
    as cornering in *shōgi*

炭團いけて雪隠詰の工夫哉
*tadon ikete setchinzume no kufū kana*

a fork in the road
    ugh! flayed by the cold

追分で引き剝がれたる寒かな
*oiwake de hikihagaretaru samusa kana*

so easily
    you squeezed the child out
        like a sea slug

安々と海鼠の如き子を生めり
*yasuyasu to namako no gotoki ko o umeri*[10]

tea ceremony
  the intermittent rain dissuades the guests

茶の會に客の揃はぬ時雨哉
*cha no kai ni kyaku no sorowanu shigure kana*

silver and gold adorn the casket
  nothing cold about it

白金に黄金に柩寒からず
*shirogane ni kogane ni hitsugi samukarazu*

though withering winds may have urged them down
  there were none that blew

凩の下にゐろとも吹かぬなり
*kogarashi no shita ni iro tomo fukanu nari*

a withering wind;
  it quieted down for the Imperial hearse

凩や吹き靜まつて喪の車
*kogarashi ya fukishizumatte mo no kuruma*

snapped by the teeth of wooden clogs;
    frost spires

ほきとをる下駄の歯形や霜柱
*hokito oru geta no hagata ya shimobashira*

the color of railing post caps in the moonlight;
    melting frost

月にうつる擬寶珠の色やとくる霜
*tsuki ni utsuru giboshi no iro ya tokuru shimo*

only the mountain bandit's face is lit
    glowing kindling flames

山賊の顔のみ明かき榾火かな
*sanzoku no kao nomi akaki hotabi kana*

on the flower vender
    cold pearl earrings

花賣に寒し眞珠の耳飾
*hanauri ni samushi shinju no mimikazari*

ascending to the third floor to sleep alone
   the cold

三階に獨り寐に行く寒かな
*sankai ni hitori ne ni yuku samusa kana*

roused from slumber
   a weasel darts out from beneath the brush clover

扶け起す萩の下より鼬かな
*tasukeokosu hagi no shita yori itachi kana*

striking the black wall;
   my sister's snowball

黒塀にあたるや妹が雪礫
*kurobei ni ataru ya imo ga yukitsubute*

a little girl and a young man;
   a snowball

女の童に小冠者一人や雪礫
*me no warawa ni kokaja hitori ya yukitsubute*

what calls this murder of crows?
  desolate field

むら鴉何に集る枯野かな
*muragarasu nani ni atsumaru kareno kana*

folding an umbrella
  the heft of the snow;
    public bath entrance

たゝむ傘に雪の重みや湯屋の門
*tatamu kasa ni yuki no omomi ya yuya no kado*

my shadow blown across a long desolate field

吾影の吹かれて長き枯野哉
*waga kage no fukarete nagaki kareno kana*

surviving embarrasses me;
  frost at my temples

生殘る吾恥かしや鬢の霜
*ikinokoru ware hazukashi ya bin no shimo*[11]

ask the wind
   which leaves shall scatter first?

風に聞け何れか先に散る木の葉
*kaze ni kike izure ka saki ni chiru konoha*

---

a stand of cedars concealing a temple
   sporadic rain

杉木立寺を藏して時雨けり
*sugi kodachi tera o kakushite shigurekeri*

---

the pop, pop of grilling tofu on a skewer
   early winter rain

豆腐燒く串にはらはら時雨哉
*tōfu yaku kushi ni harahara shigure kana*

---

have them bring the *shonzui* porcelain
   magnolias on the verandah

祥瑞を持てこさせ縁に辛夷哉
*shonzui o motekosase en ni kobushi kana*[12]

WINTER

loading a horse on a boat
willows at the ferry landing

馬を船に乗せて柳の渡哉
*uma o fune ni nosete yanagi no watashi kana*

a nightingale;
a lone straw raincoat diving through a thicket

鶯や藪くゞり行く蓑一つ
*uguisu ya yabu kuguriyuku mino hitotsu*

# No Season

# 無

even Saigyō doffs his hat and looks
    Mount Fuji

西行も笠ぬいで見る富士の山
*Saigyō mo kasa nuide miru Fuji no yama*[1]

---

myriad white clouds;
    crawl around mountains piled upon mountains

白雲や山叉山を這ひ回
*shirakumo ya yama mata yama o haimawari*

## Lamentations for a Wife

your mortal lifetime
    at but twenty-five years old
      cut short

人生を廿五年に縮めけり
*jinsei o nijū-go nen ni chijimekeri*[2]

## Lamentations for a Wife

bones;
    these, too, are a beauty's lot

骸骨や是も美人のなれの果
*gaikotsu ya kore mo bijin no nare no hate*[3]

capriciously comes Death
    regret fills the world

何となう死に來た世の惜まるゝ
*nan to nō shi ni kita yo no oshimaruru*

to the nunnery;
　　come visit this untonsured acolyte

尼寺に有髪の僧を尋ね來よ
*amadera ni yūatsu no sō o tazunekoyo*

flowing water
　　morning or night!
　　　　such vitality

ゆく水の朝な夕なに忙しき
*yuku mizu no asa na yū na ni isogashiki*

smokey water haze up from the base of the falls
　　a frightful tempest

水烟る瀑の底より嵐かな
*mizu keburu taki no soko yori arashi kana*

## Expressing my desire for you to come visit me as I lie here, ill with the excesses of debauchery.

if neither wine nor women suffice
blossoms or the moon

酒に女御意に召さずば花に月
*sake ni onna gyoi ni mesazuba hana ni tsuki*

---

Kasugano field
thoroughly burned
right down to the cow dung

春日野は牛の糞まで焼てけり
*Kasugano wa ushi no fun made yaketekeri*

---

arranging flowers
how captivating the Kyoto lilt from an unwed lass

花を活けて京音の寡婦なまめかし
*hana o ikete kyōon no kafu namamekashi*

## NO SEASON

the wind blows
   a hanging wisteria family crest on the curtain

風が吹く幕の御紋は下り藤
*kaze ga fuku maku no gomon wa sagarifuji*

streaming sunlight;
   a mood warm as a ripe persimmon

日あたりや熟柿の如き心地あり
*hiatari ya jukushi no gotoki kokochi ari*

is that the rain I hear with such melancholy?
   nighttime attendants

蕭々の雨と聞くらん宵の伽
*shōshō no ame to kikuran yoi no togi*

# Notes

## The New Year Notes

1  Sōseki may be referencing a poem attributed to the famously irreverent Zen Buddhist monk and poet Ikkyū Sōjun (1394–1481): *yami no yo ni nakanu karasu no koe kikeba umarenu saki no chichi zo koishiki* on a dark night / when I hear / a non-cawing crow / o! how I long / for my father ere he was born. Alternatively, when students of Zen are directed to meditate on his origins, trying to visualize his parents as they were before he was born is one route toward this goal.

2  Ogata Kōrin (1658–1716) was a painter best known for his folding screens decorated with flowers, particularly Irises.

3  Sōseki may be alluding to a Zen *kōan* by Wumen Huikai (1183–1260), a Song Dynasty (960–1279) Chan master who compiled the 48-*kōan* collection *The Gateless Barrier* (*Wumenguan*) in 1228. Two monks were arguing over a waving flag. One claimed the flag was moving; the other countered the wind was moving. The Sixth Patriarch rebuked them both, saying it was the mind that was moving.

4  Kohōgen was the posthumous name of Muromachi-era (1336–1573) painter Kanō Motonobu (1476–1559), the first child of the founder of the Kanō School, Kanō Masanobu (ca. 1434–ca. 1530).

## Spring Notes

1  Referencing Du Fu's (712–770) "Eight Immortals of the Wine Cup," specifically He Zhizhang (ca. 659–744), a poet and scholar-official.

2  Hikaru Genji, the protagonist of *The Tale of Genji* (c. 1005), exiled himself to Suma for a year (ch. 12) in an effort to escape the damage to his reputation he had suffered as a consequence of his sexual dalliances coming to light.

3  Sōseki is referencing a story in the great war tale *Heike monogatari* in which Kumagae no Jirō Naozane finds, upon killing the Taira warrior Atsumori, a fine flute named Saeda, an alternative name for which is *Aoba* ("green leaf") and which is preserved at Sumadera Temple in Kobe.

4  Sōseki is probably referencing the *nō* drama *Ataka* (1465) or its kabuki version, *Kanjinchō* (1840).

5  A reference to a proverb: "An apprentice near a temple will recite the scriptures untaught" or "We are products of our environment."

6  Sakata Kinpira was the heroic protagonist of the Kinpira *jōruri* plays, particularly popular in Edo and originating in the 1600s.

7  Imadoyaki is a style of unglazed pottery and, as it probably is here, a metaphor for a homely woman.

8  Ryōunkaku, the "Cloud-Surpassing Pavilion," was a 12-story brick edifice built

## NOTES

in Asakusa, Tokyo, which, from 1890 to 1923, stood as Japan's first western-style skyscraper. The pleasures it offered to the populace—it featured theatres, restaurants, and bars on every floor—as well as its unique aspects, including the first elevator in Japan, ensured that it would quickly become a major tourist destination.

9 Sōseki is, perhaps, engaging in allusive variation here, playing on a poem by Sone no Yoshitada (*fl.* latter 10c), one of the Thirty-six Immortals of Poetry, anthologized in the eighth imperial collection of poetry, the *Shinkokinwakashū* (New collection of poems ancient and modern, c. 1205): *Yura no to o wataru funabito kaji o tae yukue mo shiranu koi no michi kana* over the Yura Strait / drift fishermen / oarless / toward the unknown / as I am / on the path of love.

10 Takahama Kyoshi (1874–1959) was a poet and novelist who lived in Matsuyama and who had studied under Masaoka Shiki. He became one of the most influential *haiku* poets of his time, and established a publishing firm focusing on *haiku*. Murakami Seigetsu (c. 1871–1946) was another poet who lived in Matsuyama and who had studied under Shiki.

11 Kanzan (C: Hanshan; *fl.* 9th century) was a recluse poet about whom very little is certain. Jittoku (C: Shide; *fl.* 9th century) was a legendary Chinese poet-priest of the Tang Dynasty, and was associated with Guoqing Temple on Mount Tiantai in Taizhou, Zhejiang Province, China.

12 Characterized by soft brushstrokes, *nanga* ("southern painting") was associated with literati painting in the eighteenth and nineteenth centuries.

13 The three sages are Confucius, Laozi, and the Buddha.

14 Presumably composed when Sōseki visited some place associated with the Taira Clan whose battle standard was red (in contradistinction to the Minamoto, whose standard was white).

15 Yoshida Kenkō (1283–1350) was an author and Buddhist monk.

16 In March 1898, Sōseki's influential friend Masaoka Shiki published a collection of *haiku* entitled *Shin haiku* (New *haiku*) and had sent a copy to Sōseki.

17 Ike no Gyokuran (1727–84) and her husband, Ike no Taiga (1723–76), were both Kyoto calligraphers and *nanga* ("southern painting") artists.

18 "Old plum grove" is also the name of one brand of India ink.

19 Shashunsei was one of the *noms de plume* used by noted *haiku* poet Yosa Buson (1716–84) when he was painting.

20 There is speculation that one stanza in the poem "I stood tip-toe upon a little hill" by John Keats (1795–1821) occasioned this burst of admiration.

21 Kusamakura (1906) was Sōseki's third novel. Two English translations exist. Hirose Izen (d. 1711) was a *haiku* poet and disciple of Matsuo Bashō (1644–94).

22 Nomura Denshi (1880–1948) was a student of Sōseki's who went on to become a teacher and head of the Nara Prefectural Library.

23 Sōseki refers to a line from the auspicious *nō* play "Takasago" by Zeami Motokiyo (ca. 1363–ca. 1443).

24 Isoda Taka (1879–1945) was a *geisha* in the Gion entertainment district of Kyoto and the proprietress of the Daitomo teahouse. Her associations with promi-

*283*

# SŌSEKI NATSUME'S COLLECTED HAIKU

nent figures in the world of letters earned her the nickname of "the literary *geisha*."
25 Shizue was the daughter of Takita Choin (1882–1925), publisher of the magazine *Chūō kōron*.

## Summer Notes

1 Yan Ying (c. 578–500 BCE), better known as Yan Zi, was an accomplished philosopher and statesman during the Spring and Autumn Period (c. 771–476 BCE) in China.

2 A *koku* was a measure of rice equal to about 330 pounds. It was often used to describe the wealth of a retainer's or lord's domain. Sōseki is probably riffing on a popular song with the following lyrics: "Shall I sleep with you or shall I take 5,000 *koku*? What's 5,000 *koku*? I'll sleep with you!"

3 Sokuhi Nyoitsu (1616–71) was a Chinese Buddhist monk and a poet and calligrapher who travelled to Japan in 1657, staying there until his death. Sokuhi is also a philosophical term meaning "is and is not."

4 The Japanese adopted the Chinese folk wisdom practice of bathing in hot water infused with orchid leaves on Boys' Day (5 May) to ward off evil spirits.

5 Tabaruzaka was the site of a major battle in the Satsuma Rebellion in March 1877.

6 Wen Yuke was the style name of the 11th-century Northern Song painter Wen Tong (1019–1079) famed for his bamboo paintings in charcoal ink.

7 Although *zatsuei* are poems (notably, *haiku*) without a specific theme, Sōseki has chosen to provide a context for all of the poems in this series.

8 Here, the capital is London.

9 Monogusa Tarō is a character in a medieval *otogizōshi* (shorter prose narrative) tale who goes from poverty to wealth, a common theme in *otogizōshi*. Sōseki is undoubtedly being ironic as his time in London was marked by a degree of penury.

10 Sōseki might be alluding to an 1893 poem by Masaoka Shiki: *hadakami no kabe ni hittsuku atsusa kana* my naked body pressed against the wall / what heat!

## Autumn Notes

1 Sōseki's sister-in-law, Tose, the second wife of his elder brother, Wasaburō, died of *hyperemesis gravidarum* (morning sickness) on 28 July 1891.

2 Sōseki's sister-in-law, Tose, the second wife of his elder brother, Wasaburō, died of *hyperemesis gravidarum* (morning sickness) on 28 July 1891.

3 Traditionally, the larvae of bagworm moths are said to utter their plaintive cry when the winds marking the end of autumn blow. This cry of *chichi yo, chichi yo*—"o, father; o, father"—has associations with the pathos accompanying the transition from fall to winter.

4 The Chinese Jin Dynasty is traditionally dated 266–420 CE. Sōseki may be alluding to the Seven Sages of the Bamboo Grove.

5 *The Blue Cliff Record* is a collection of Zen Buddhist *kōan*, originally compiled in China in 1125.

# NOTES

6  Now known as Xi'an, Chang'an was the ancient Chinese capital intermittently for many centuries from c. 1046 BCE to 904 CE. It was the model for Kyoto.

7  The *shōgyōjō* was a rubbing copy of the *shōgyōnojo* (Preface to the sacred writings) by Wang Xizhi (303–361), one of the greatest calligraphers in Chinese history. It was carved into his gravestone and is used as a model for calligraphy.

8  Koharu and Jihei were the two ill-fated lovers who committed a double suicide in Osaka at Daichōji Temple in 1720. Edo-period dramatist Chikamatsu Monzaemon (1653–1725) imortalized their story in the *bunraku* play *Shinjuten no amijima* (Love Suicide at Amijima, 1720), but the incident has served as grist for other creative mills, as well.

9  Fujino Kohaku, a poet, dramatist, and novelist, was Masaoka Shiki's cousin. He committed suicide on 12 April 1895.

10  Heike crabs have markings on their shells reminiscent of faces. Legend has it that they are the faces of the myriad Heike clan warriors who died in the Inland Sea.

11  Although the specifics are not quite accurate, Sōseki would appear to be referencing the Battle of Feishui (383), an incident in which the Eastern Jin (266–420) soldiers were fighting a vastly superior Former Qin Dynasty (351–394) army, yet were able to claim victory though deception. They made the opposing soldiers believe that the wind in the trees and the honking of cranes were the sounds of soldiers in hot pursuit during the disorganized katabasis of the Former Qin troops.

12  A Guan shrine celebrates Guan Yu (d. 220), a Chinese general active at the end of the Han Dynasty (206 BCE–220 CE) and beginning of the Three Kingdoms era (220–80) in China. He is the embodiment of loyalty and righteousness and was eventually seen as a god.

13  Although *zatsuei* are poems (notably, *haiku*) without a specific theme, Sōseki has chosen to provide a context for all of the poems in this series.

14  Sōseki may be alluding to a 1692 *hokku* by Matsuo Bashō (1644–94): *aokute mo arubeki mono o tōgarashi* (green it should have stayed / red pepper).

15  The general Fan Kuai (c. 242–c. 189 BCE) was an important figure in the establishment of the early Western Han Dynasty (206 BCE–9 CE).

16  Shen Quan (1682–1760), whose courtesy name was Nanpin, was a Qing Dynasty painter known for his particularly realistic style of painting. Shen spent two years in Japan, during which time he had numerous students and a significant effect on the "bird-and-flower" (*kachōga*) genre in Japan.

17  This and the following two poems were written on hearing of the death of Masaoka Shiki who died on 19 September 1902.

18  Located in the coastal region of northern Kyoto Prefecture, Amanohashidate is a pine-covered sandbar about two miles in length. It is considered one of Japan's three scenic views.

19  This poem, and the next four, are from *Travels in Manchuria and Korea* (*Mankan tokorodokoro*, 1909), a record of Sōseki's journey to these Japanese colonies with

*285*

Nakamura Yoshikoto (1867–1927), Chairman of the South Manchurian Railway Company.

20  Sōseki is playing on the name of Higuchi Dōgyū (1866–1932), the author of *Haikai shin kenkyū* (1909; New research on *haikai*). Dōgyū, means "copper bull."

21  Sōseki had a life-threatening stomach illness in 1910 and betook himself to Shuzenji hot spring to recuperate.

22  Minamoto no Noriyori (1150–93) was a late-Heian-era general who fought in the Genpei War (1180–85). His brother and Shōgun, Minamoto Yoritomo (1147–99), eventually ordered his death for conspiracy. He was killed at Shuzenji.

23  Yoshida Zōtaku (1722–1802) was a painter renowned for his bamboo renderings in India ink.

24  Mizuochi Roseki (1872–1919) was a *haiku* poet from Osaka who studied under Masaoka Shiki.

25  Sōseki had just had surgery for hemorrhoids.

## Winter Notes

1  Musashibō Benkei (d. 1189) is a legendary warrior who, in an attempt to get the last of 1,000 swords from passersby he challenged to a duel, fought a battle on Go-jō Bridge with Ushiwakamaru (later known as Minamoto Yoshitsune [1159–89]), lost, and became the latter's devoted right-hand man.

2  "The thirty-six mountains" is an appellation applied to the mountain range east and south of Kyoto.

3  A traditional art involving the construction of clothing out of sturdy paper fibers.

4  Here, Seto denotes a particular style of pottery and glaze.

5  Minamoto no Noriyori (1150–93) was a late-Heian-era general who fought in the Genpei War (1180–85). His brother and Shōgun, Minamoto Yoritomo (1147–99), eventually ordered his death for conspiracy.

6  A section of Tokyo once famed for the dwellings of lords and retainers, and subsequently known in the Meiji era for its high-end homes.

7  Wei Shuzi was a pen name of Wei Xi (1624–81), one of three major essayists of the Qing Dynasty. The "Great Iron Hammer" was the nickname of a brave knight-errant in one of Wei's stories who, in a single battle, defeated over thirty foes with his formidable iron hammer.

8  Located in the mountains of Kumamoto Prefecture, Kyushu, Goka-no-shō was the final hiding place of the Taira clan at the end of the Genpei War (1180–85).

9  See Autumn note 15 that also references Fan Kuai.

10  Written on the occasion of the birth of Sōseki's eldest daughter.

11  Both Sōseki's eldest brother, Daisuke (1856–87), and his next eldest brother, Einosuke (1858–87), died of consumption in the prime of life.

12  Shonzui is a brown-rimmed, blue-and-white porcelain, dating originally from the end of the Ming (1368–1644) and beginning of Qing (1644–1911) dynasties, and eventually produced in Japan in the Tokugawa period (1600–1868).

# NOTES

**No Season Notes**

1 Saigyō Hōshi (西行法師, 1118–90). A famed poet monk known for the poetry he wrote on numerous long journeys.

2 Sōseki's sister-in-law, Tose, the second wife of his elder brother, Wasaburō, died of *hyperemesis gravidarum* (morning sickness) on 28 July 1891.

3 Sōseki's sister-in-law, Tose, the second wife of his elder brother, Wasaburō, died of *hyperemesis gravidarum* (morning sickness) on 28 July 1891.

**Photo Credits**

**Author's photos:** pp. ii, iv, vii, xiii

**Shutterstock photos:** p. 3 ©Hyeonkyu Park; p. 12 ©f11photo; p. 33 ©Christine Summers; p. 59 ©Taromon; p. 75 ©Budimm; p. 92 ©Jennifer Jensen; p. 98 ©Bill Chizek; p. 103 ©Smutan; p. 110 ©Evion Lim; p. 118 ©beeboys; p. 155 ©Shyjo; p. 164 ©Martin Gstoehl; p. 277 ©KorradolYamsatthm

**Dreamstime photos:** ends (front & back) ©Ennjee; p. 131 ©Martin Kobsch; pp. 139 and 146 ©Taras Vyshnya

## "Books to Span the East and West"

**Tuttle Publishing** was founded in 1832 in the small New England town of Rutland, Vermont [USA]. Our core values remain as strong today as they were then—to publish best-in-class books which bring people together one page at a time. In 1948, we established a publishing outpost in Japan—and Tuttle is now a leader in publishing English-language books about the arts, languages and cultures of Asia. The world has become a much smaller place today and Asia's economic and cultural influence has grown. Yet the need for meaningful dialogue and information about this diverse region has never been greater. Over the past seven decades, Tuttle has published thousands of books on subjects ranging from martial arts and paper crafts to language learning and literature—and our talented authors, illustrators, designers and photographers have won many prestigious awards. We welcome you to explore the wealth of information available on Asia at **www.tuttlepublishing.com**.

Published by Tuttle Publishing, an imprint of Periplus Editions (HK) Ltd.

**www.tuttlepublishing.com**

Copyright ©2024 Periplus Editions (HK) Ltd

All rights reserved. No part of this publication may be reproduced or utilized in any form or by any means, electronic or mechanical, including photocopying, recording, or by any information storage and retrieval system, without prior written permission from the publisher.

ISBN: 978-4-8053-1845-4

**Distributed by**

| North America, Latin America & Europe | Japan | Asia Pacific |
|---|---|---|
| Tuttle Publishing | Tuttle Publishing | Berkeley Books Pte Ltd |
| 364 Innovation Drive | Yaekari Building | 3 Kallang Sector #04-01 |
| North Clarendon | 3rd Floor, 5-4-12 Osaki | Singapore 349278 |
| VT 05759-9436 U.S.A. | Shinagawa-ku | Tel: (65) 6741 2178 |
| Tel: 1 (802) 773-8930 | Tokyo 141 0032 | Fax: (65) 6741 2179 |
| Fax: 1 (802) 773-6993 | Tel: (81) 3 5437-0171 | inquiries@periplus.com.sg |
| info@tuttlepublishing.com | Fax: (81) 3 5437-0755 | www.tuttlepublishing.com |
| www.tuttlepublishing.com | sales@tuttle.co.jp | |
| | www.tuttle.co.jp | |

28 27 26 25        10 9 8 7 6 5 4 3 2 1        2501CM
Printed in China

TUTTLE PUBLISHING® is a registered trademark of Tuttle Publishing, a division of Periplus Editions (HK) Ltd.